navigate toxic relationships—inside their home and outside it, too—this book offers clarity, hope, and a carefully discerned road map on how best to move forward. Melanie is living proof that a healthy family can come from you, even if you don't come from a healthy family—and that peace is possible when God is your guide. I found myself crying and cheering for Melanie and her daughter as they learned to stand up for themselves, stop the mean-girl cycle, and still choose kindness. The generational impact of *Here Be Dragons* can't be overstated."

—KARI KAMPAKIS, author of *Love Her Well* and host of the *Girl Mom* podcast

"It's no secret that Melanie and I are close friends—we've done a podcast together for an obnoxious number of years, after all—and that is how I know that this isn't the book Melanie intended to write. She planned to write primarily about the importance of healing, without focusing too much on the pain of the breaking. But as Melanie started to unearth the layers of her own story, it was clear to those of us who know her best that the Lord was giving her fresh compassion, not just for what she experienced in her own family but also for the ways generational wounds can linger in so many of our lives. Melanie responded to this compassion with courage and candor, and as a result, you are going to see a side of her life you have likely not known before. While it may break your heart a little bit, this book will also make you laugh, will challenge you, and will point you again and again to the Source of our hope and redemption. *Here Be Dragons* is Melanie's very best writing to date: honest, tender, and full of hope. I'm so proud of her for sharing this part of her story. We're so fortunate that we get to read it."

—SOPHIE HUDSON, co-host of *The Big Boo Cast* and bestselling author of *A Fine Sight to See*

HERE BE
DRAGONS

HERE BE DRAGONS

Treading the Deep Waters of Motherhood,
Mean Girls, and Generational Trauma

WaterBrook

Library of Congress Cataloging-in-Publication Data
Names: Shankle, Melanie, author.
Title: Here be dragons: treading the deep waters of motherhood, mean girls, and
generational trauma / Melanie Shankle.
Description: Colorado Springs: WaterBrook, 2025. | Includes bibliographical references.
Identifiers: LCCN 2024018791 | ISBN 9780593601204 (hardcover) |
ISBN 9780593601211 (ebook)
Subjects: LCSH: Mothers and daughters—Religious aspects—Christianity. |
Intergenerational communication—Religious aspects—Christianity.
Classification: LCC BV4529.18 .S49 2025 | DDC 248.8/431—dc23/eng/20241115
LC record available at https://lccn.loc.gov/2024018791

To Caroline:

I would say you are the best parts of me, and perhaps that is accurate. But you are so much more than that. You are a warrior, a wisdom seeker, and one of the funniest people I know. Being your mom is the greatest gift I've been given. I know I haven't done it perfectly, but I've done it with more love, intention, and admiration than you will ever know. Keep chasing after Jesus; He will always be the one who gives us the strength to fight the dragons and loves us back to health.

You own everything that happened to you. Tell your stories. If people wanted you to write warmly about them, they should have behaved better.

—Anne Lamott, *Bird by Bird*

CONTENTS

INTRODUCTION

I've been sitting here staring at a cursor blinking on my laptop screen for the better part of an hour. Actually, for the better part of a year. It's been almost four years since I've written a book, and I'm afraid I've forgotten how. Or maybe I remember and realize now exactly how difficult it's going to be. Once, I was a naïve, bright-eyed young author who jumped in with both feet. But after writing six books in eight years, I'm the author equivalent of an old lady yelling at kids to get off my lawn and then posting on Nextdoor about it. *Also, are those fireworks or gunshots?*

The truth is, I haven't even been sure that I would write another book. I'm at an age where I prefer to leave hard things to the youngsters. I've done my time. First Ecclesiastes references toiling endlessly in the sun (verse 3), and that is a young woman's game. I have enough sun damage.

The past few years have found me at a new stage in life. My daughter, Caroline, just finished her sophomore year of college, and I've officially been an empty nester for almost two years. I think it was the fastest period of my life. It's given me time to reflect on where I've been as a mother and a woman and where I'm headed, even though at age fifty-two, I continue to have days when I feel as though I'm still searching for a life vision.

Way back in ye olden days of 2015, I wrote a book called *Nobody's Cuter than You.* It's a memoir about friendship and essentially a love letter to all the great girlfriends I've been fortunate to have over the course of my life. Some of those relationships were just for a season, and some of those friends continue to be my ride-or-die girls, but they all shaped me in some way. And to this day, *Nobody's Cuter than You* continues to sell really well. I could show you the sales numbers, but then you would be depressed at how few people actually buy books and read them, so I'll spare you that knowledge. Let's just say that 99.99 percent of all authors are not J. K. Rowling. But if anyone would like to license and build a Nobody's Cuter than You theme park, please call me.

Anyway, when I wrote that book, Caroline was twelve years old, just on the cusp of her teen years. We hadn't yet experienced any of the mean-girl dynamics that people had warned me about. In fact, she'd made it all the way through seventh grade fairly unscathed. I thought that maybe her teen years were going to be easier than I'd been led to believe. Plus, I'd written an entire book on female friendship, which made me an expert for guiding her through high school, right?

Let's say it together: "Aw, buddy."

If the past several years have taught us anything, it's that we never know what twists and turns we will face and what challenges lie ahead. And I will tell you, I wasn't prepared for what brand of Hades high school would wreak on my girl. I found myself floundering, seeking solutions that wouldn't come, and searching for that buried treasure of parenthood known as having the right answers. I'd never been more in need of some sort of map to show the way or more aware that no such map was available. Parenting is life's equivalent of a pop quiz in the hardest class covering a topic that was covered on a day you chose to sleep in. Which is to say, we are all just, in the words of Bon Jovi, "livin' on a prayer."[1]

I'm not any sort of expert in ancient mapmaking, but there are stories about cartographers during medieval times who marked maps with the Latin phrase *Hc svnt dracones*, which translates to "Here be dragons." That phrase signified uncharted waters and unexplored territories where no one knew what dangers might lie ahead. Essentially, our whole life could be marked "Here be dragons" because we never know for sure what is waiting ahead.

The August right before Caroline started her sophomore year in high school, she was playing in her first soccer tournament of the club season when she took a ball right to the face. Her nose immediately began to gush blood, and she had to run to the sideline because there are rules about bleeding on the field. I watched from the far sideline as she held a towel to her nose and wondered if she'd just messed up thousands of dollars in orthodontia and if I needed to take her to the emergency room. About that time, she changed into a teammate's clean jersey, ran back onto the field like nothing had ever happened, and proceeded to score two goals to close out the game.

Little did we know then that getting nailed in the face with a soccer ball was basically going to be a metaphor for the rest of her high school years. I realize now that moment was what we call foreshadowing, and the following years were ones I don't think I'll ever forget. When people ask me about the hardest years of my life, I'll say, "High school," and I won't mean my own high school years; I'll mean hers. It's painful to watch the person you love more than anything fight difficult battles that you can't fight for her. You feel every bit of it so deeply yet are powerless to make anything better.

Those were the years when Caroline had to learn to stand strong for what she knew was right, even when it meant she might be alone as she stood up to mean girls. She had to make tough decisions about what is worth fighting for and when it's time to walk away. She learned that life isn't always fair and things don't always work out the way you think they should. She figured out that sometimes the only prize for making the right decisions is the peace that comes with knowing you did. She also figured out that maybe she needed to filter some of her thoughts and that she wasn't always right. And I had to do my best to parent every inch of that while also allowing her to learn how to stand on her own.

What I didn't know at the beginning of this whole journey was the ways parenting would cause me to have to continue to heal and deal with my own past and the baggage I'd carried along the way. It was a catalyst that made me realize that the first mean girl I ever faced was my own mother.

Can you say "generational trauma"? I knew you could.

I prayed since the day Caroline was born that God would make her strong, confident, and brave. I just didn't think about the dragons she'd have to conquer to forge those characteristics. I didn't realize the bridges that would have to be burned and the healing that God would have to continue to do in my own life so my child could grow up in an emotionally healthy environment and become a strong, independent, well-adjusted woman in her own right.

Caroline took a lot of hits, and it was hard to watch even though I knew those were the very things that were making her into the person God meant for her to become. And isn't that the reality every mother of a teen girl experiences as we watch our girls struggle with friendship dynamics, painful breakups, and all the other obstacles they will face on this precipice of adulthood? A mother's heart is stitched together with the most tender of materials, so we feel everything. Every tear, every struggle, every injustice. And I believe that it all gets amplified because we were once teen girls ourselves. Don't you remember how terrible and wonderful it could be (sometimes all in a twenty-four-hour period)?

It's hard to bring up a warrior who fights dragons rather than a princess who gets rescued. Dragons are terrifying to face, but they can destroy everything in their paths if allowed to remain. It's a lot messier and not nearly as pretty as the fairy tale. But our girls have got to be resilient because the world will knock them down and tell them all the ways they aren't good enough or smart enough and all the reasons they should lower their expectations.

And here's the thing I witnessed during her high school years that I first saw a glimpse of during that soccer game when she ran back onto the field: Caroline never quit getting back in the game. She took her hits, wiped off the blood and tears, and got back up over and over again, even though sometimes she got a little belligerent with both the referees and her parents. Meanwhile, I did my best to cheer her on, pray like I'd never prayed before, and equip her to fight the dragons she encoun-tered. My husband, Perry, and I trusted God every step of the way and did our best to point her to Him in every aspect of her life—without quashing the strong-willed parts of her personal-ity, but helping her soften some of the rough edges. And I can say with all confidence that He never once let us down, even when things didn't look like we'd hoped or planned.

In the map of my life, the gift of raising Caroline has been my greatest adventure and a reminder that the dragons you face will make you stronger and more resilient than you could have ever imagined before you found yourself among them. This is how you become a warrior. This is how you raise a warrior. Perry has a tender saying that you are welcome to print out and hang in your home: "If you don't deal with your sh%$, it's going to come out sideways." Ultimately, this book is the story of the sh%$ I had to live through, heal from, and overcome to become a healthy woman, wife, mom, and friend. It's about the cycles we must break if we don't want them repeated.

As you'll see in the pages that follow, leaving behind the dys-function I was born into to become some version of what God made me to be has challenged me to my core. My prayer is that this book can serve as some sort of map if you've found yourself in the midst of the uncharted waters of raising a teenager, heal-ing from your own emotional wounds, and wondering if you can possibly survive it.

Spoiler alert: You can. And you will.

HERE BE
DRAGONS

CHAPTER 1

Let's Begin Our Journey

Something permanently shifted in me the day I found out we were having a girl. A daughter. Somewhere deep inside me I'd suspected we were going to have a daughter. I'd even bought a couple of pink dresses. But it was the confirmation of the ultrasound technician pointing out the telltale signs and declaring, "Congrats! You're having a girl!" that changed me forever. I knew two things for certain at that moment: I'd never wanted anything more than I wanted a daughter, and I was terrified to be the mother of a daughter.

Perry and I drove home, excitedly talking about our girl, who now felt officially like a reality. We'd had a long road to get to this point: a miscarriage that turned out to be a molar pregnancy, months of blood draws and eventually injections to get my body back to normal, and then finding out I was pregnant about two months earlier than the doctor had advised was safe for my body. Apparently, there really is no such thing as safe sex, so let that be a lesson to you, children. It really does take only one time to get pregnant.

And then, even after the doctor confirmed I was pregnant, there were concerns about my hormone levels and my ability to carry a baby to term. The nights I lay in bed with my hand over my stomach and prayed God would let this baby live were countless. All that to say, to reach the twenty-week mark and see an ultrasound of a healthy baby girl with impossibly long legs moving around inside me felt like nothing short of a miracle. What felt substantially less wonderful were all the thoughts and doubts swirling in my head as I questioned if I would know how to raise an emotionally healthy girl. Would God give me the strength and wisdom and fortitude to break the unhealthy cycle I'd come from? Would I be able to recognize patterns and behavior that had caused so much brokenness in me and stemmed from the relationship I had with my mother?

A few weeks after that ultrasound—as we continued to debate naming our baby Caroline, Olivia, or Kate—I was sitting in a church service in a small garden chapel. Everyone around me was standing up and singing worship songs, but I'd had to sit down because those aforementioned long legs of my baby girl were engaged in a game of kickball with my bladder and I felt like I was about to wet my pants in front of a bunch of Methodists. I don't mean to glamorize pregnancy in this way, but this is the truth. Don't hate the player; hate the game.

In an attempt to distract myself from the tiny foot wedged beneath my rib cage, I picked up the Bible that was in the pew rack in front of me. I was just kind of thumbing through it when I stopped at Isaiah 44 and read,

I will pour water on the thirsty land,
    and streams on the dry ground;

I will pour my Spirit upon your offspring,
and my blessing on your descendants.
They shall spring up among the grass
like willows by flowing streams.
This one will say, "I am the LORD's." (verses 3–5, ESV)

I knew that God had led me to those specific words to assure
me that He saw me and had heard my whispered midnight
inquiries asking Him if I was up for all that was ahead of me.
I'd spent most of my life feeling all the ramifications of coming
from a relationship with my mom that often felt barren and
cold, yet there was God promising to pour out His Spirit and
blessings on this new life that was clearly in a gang fight with
my bladder.

A few months later, Caroline Tatum Shankle arrived. In a
move that turned out to be so indicative of her entire personality, she arrived two weeks early and barely made a sound as they
suctioned out her lungs, cleaned her up, swaddled her in a blanket, and handed her to me. She just stared at me with eyes that
never seemed to blink, like she was sizing me up and deciding
if I was up for the job of being her mother. I thought, *Honestly,
kid, we'll see. I thought the labor pains were food poisoning from
eating chicken spaghetti, and I just pooped on the table while you
were being born, so I don't know that we're off to the most auspicious
of beginnings.*

Here's the thing about having a baby. You are exhausted
from labor, a little overwhelmed by everything you just realized
your body could survive, and emotionally fragile to a degree you
didn't know was possible. I mean, I ate a McDonald's McGriddles the morning after giving birth and declared it to be the

most delicious thing I'd ever eaten. Why had people been keeping the secret of the McGriddles from me? A subpar breakfast sandwich infused with the flavor of maple syrup brought tears to my eyes.

Friends who'd already had babies had told me to let the nurses occasionally take the infant back to the nursery so I could get some sleep, and this turned out to be solid advice. For twenty-four hours after giving birth, I had sweet nurses who brought Caroline to me and showed me what to do. They gave me ice packs to sit on and mesh panties that should be Victoria's real secret. And then, just as I was kind of settling in, they told me it was time for Perry and me to take our baby and go home. Just the three of us. It was harder for me to get a job at Sound Castle Records when I was a fifteen-year-old with no résumé than it was for the hospital staff to let me leave their establishment with a human to raise to adulthood.

That first week home went by in a blur of diaper blowouts, swaddling attempts, and my boobs feeling like they might explode. The details of that time are a little foggy from the viewpoint of twenty years later, but I vividly remember one night as I was rocking Caroline in her pink nursery after a late feeding that I hoped would mean both of us would sleep for at least three hours. I looked down at this unimaginable beauty wrapped up in my arms with her milk-drunk face and knew I'd never loved anything more. She was my whole heart in a petal-pink blanket. And because I like to worry about things way in advance, I began at that very second to dread the day I'd have to send her to kindergarten. Which led to my thinking about the day she would inevitably graduate from high school, and I genuinely prayed that perhaps Jesus would return before I had to deal with that milestone. There was no way I could ever bear to not always have her with me. How would I ever be able to let her go?

And it was right after I'd had this flood of concerns that another realization hit me in such a way that it almost made me physically hurt.

I knew at that moment that my own mother had never loved me like I loved this baby.

I mean, don't misunderstand. I knew that my mom loved me. But when I was growing up, we always seemed to be in this precarious dance of wills and resentment, admiration and jealousy. Rather than feeling her unconditional love, I always felt that my mom's affection was dependent on my being exactly what she wanted me to be, often at the expense of my own needs and feelings.

As I looked at my little girl and thought about my mom, I knew that the only thing I wanted for my baby was for her to find the peace and joy that come with being exactly who God made her to be. I didn't want her to be a version of me, I didn't want her to be my competition, and I didn't want her to ever feel that my love for her was conditional on her ability to be a certain way. And I definitely didn't want her to bear the burden of feeling responsible for my mental outlook. That was it. It was as if I'd spent my whole life looking for a missing puzzle piece and finally found it.

CHAPTER 2

The Things Handed Down to Us

My mom, Suzanne, was a high school beauty queen. Even her name seemed impossibly glamorous for a baby born in the 1940s. She never officially held any of the desirable titles, such as homecoming or prom queen, in her small high school in the Texas Panhandle, but she assured me early on that it was only because other girls had been envious of her beauty. She was a majorette in the Floydada Whirlwinds band in the early 1960s, when the ability to twirl two batons at the same time was one of the highest aspirations a girl could possibly have. Let's not even talk about the fact that these batons were occasionally set on fire. There are some mountains in life that are too majestic for mere mortals to even consider.

Some of my earliest memories are of looking through old photo albums and her high school yearbooks, pondering if living up to my mother's glamorous standards was in the realm of possibility. Even when I was a child, she felt like a blond mystery I was always trying to solve. When we could go visit her mother, my Nanny, I would run my hand over all my mother's high school and college majorette costumes tucked away in the closet in the bedroom where I slept. The sequins, the top hats, the rhinestone fringe—in my mind, my mother had been as glamorous as Charo on a special-guest episode of *The Love Boat*. (If you were born any later than 1978, just trust me when I tell you that Charo was glamour goals and *The Love Boat* was the reason I aspired, for many of my formative years, to be a cruise director like Julie McCoy. Now I've lived enough life to know that would have been a problematic career choice because I get terribly seasick and the idea of being stuck on a boat in the middle of any ocean is one of my top five nightmares, right after biting into chicken and realizing it's raw.)

My mother came of age in the late 1950s and early 1960s, a time when teenage girls looked infinitely more glamorous and sophisticated than they did in ensuing decades. She wore gloves with her prom dresses and looked as though she'd just stepped out of a Doris Day movie. My mother's high school portraits have a dreamy quality and seem to portray a Hollywood starlet, whereas my own high school pictures taken in the late 1980s would cause today's youth to wonder if perhaps I'd once played bass guitar on "Welcome to the Jungle" for Guns N' Roses. And let me just say, "I wish."

None of my mother's achievements were by accident. Suzanne came into the world in 1946, born to a mother who valued outward appearances more than any ridiculous notion of inner beauty. Nanny was an impossibly fun, doting grandmother later in life but always a force of nature looking to bend everyone and everything in her path to her specific idea of who and what they should be. So when she gave birth to her second baby girl shortly after my grandfather returned from the Pacific at the end of World War II, she had some ambitions as to what this new daughter would be.

By the time my mother was eight years old, her older sister had married her high school sweetheart at the tender age of sixteen. Suzanne was raised as an only child for all intents and purposes and was the sole focus of all my grandmother's attention. Legend has it that Nanny still fixed my mother's hair every morning through Mom's senior year of high school to ensure she was perfectly coiffed for the day. Her dresses were handmade and portrayed a far more prosperous lifestyle than what the family bank account might reveal.

All this to say, vanity cut a deep path for the women in my family, and the quest for the fountain of youth was the river that ran through it. There was such a focus on how everything and everyone looked that it took me years to quit measuring my physical appearance against any other woman who happened to be in my vicinity. And I'm embarrassed to tell you that I have a bathroom cabinet (and several drawers) filled with all manner of potions and creams and lotions. This admission might indicate there are some things so encoded in your DNA that they may just be fundamental traits such as eye color.

And I don't know if you've ever lived in an environment that is ripe to help someone develop an eating disorder, but five minutes at my Nanny's house could do it. She valued thinness over pretty much all else and was quick to let any of the girls in our family know if they had put on a pound or two. I'll never forget one Easter break during college when my best friend, Gulley, came home with me, and Nanny felt the freedom to tell both of us, "Girls, those polka-dot dresses on that extra weight you're carrying in your behinds aren't doing you any favors." I immediately wanted to burn my beloved hot pink Leslie Lucks dress that I'd felt so great about moments before.

And, listen, you can trace all the vanity in my family line back to generations when people lived like pioneers and didn't have beauty influencers on Instagram telling them what products to buy. Years ago, when I used to write daily on my blog called *Big Mama*, several readers asked about Nanny's skin-care regimen because she looked amazing for being in her late eighties. Mind you, she'd also gotten her second facelift at the age of eighty-three, so that helped, but she still had amazing skin. I asked her if she would share her skin-care routine with my readers. The following is what she wrote:

My complexion care began at an early age—like when I was about thirteen. We didn't have clothes dryers back in those days, so we had miles of clotheslines, where we hung the wash out to dry. Maybe it had something to do with my growing taller, but it became my turn to hang the laundry out to dry.

Now, the wash consisted of tons of clothes and sheets (so many that I still have nightmares about them). I feel certain that is why I hate Mondays to this day. Everyone knew that Mondays were "wash day."

My mama, who had the most beautiful skin in Texas, allowed absolutely no sun to come in contact with her baby's precious skin—ever! Bonnets were worn from birth forward. Matter of fact, all her girl babies were probably born wearing them.

However, she did try to train me in the sharing of chores with my siblings, so there I went with a basket of freshly washed clothes and sheets. I had to wear a big bonnet with slats that extended at least twelve inches out from my face. Not one ray of sunshine was permitted on my face.

Beyond the bonnet, I was required to wear long stockings pulled up on my arms all the way to my shoulders. These "arm stockings" were pinned to my blouse along the shoulder seams.

My skin never had a freckle, much less a tan. I never learned to swim—same reason, no sun! To this day, I am terribly afraid of the water. As I mentioned before, my mother had gorgeous skin, so she taught me proper skin care. No soap (too drying)—witch-hazel (an herb or shrub of some sort, I think) ointment cleaned and was a good night cream. Later, she introduced me to Pond's cream. (Yes, it has been around a long time, and it is still good.)

Is it possible Nanny was the original beauty influencer and didn't even know it? And please note that, in the name of having beautiful skin, she never learned to swim. Girls, that is next-level commitment to skin care.

But it wasn't just vanity that ran through my maternal line for generations like a bad family heirloom that no one really wanted. At some point long before I was born, mental illness snaked its way into my family lineage and showed up in the form of alcoholism, depression, personality disorders, and suicide. My grandfather Big Bob had several sisters who self-medicated with alcohol and eventually took their own lives. I have several cousins who have struggled with both depression and bipolar disorders. I remember once asking Nanny where she got the cute trash can embellished with a poodle made from pom-poms that was in her guest bathroom. She waved her hand and nonchalantly said, "Oh, your aunt Judy made that during craft time while she was in the nuthouse back in the early seventies," as if it were just a normal stop in a person's life.

That was in the days before medication and therapy and, really, any tangible way to deal with those things, other than through vague platitudes about pulling yourself up by your bootstraps. Now that I'm old enough to understand those dynamics, I'd like to look back at our family line and study the origins of all the issues that collected over time. When did they show up? How did they get there? Was there trauma that left wounds masked with bourbon and meanness?

And here were my biggest questions that maybe you've asked yourself, too, if you come from similar family dynamics: *Is this what my future is going to be? Am I going to wake up one day and discover that I can't get out of bed? Will I end up self-medicating my pain away? Am I destined to repeat the same mistakes with my daughter that Nanny made with my mom and my mom made with me? I know I don't want this to be my future, but how can I make sure it won't be?* I've always heard people say that the best part of going crazy is that you don't know when it happens, but this scared me even more.

It's like when you develop some weird physical symptom and spend a lot of time googling things like "What does it mean if your ears itch?" and the internet basically tells you it means you're probably going to die soon. I've spent many years doing the mental equivalent of this, examining my behavior and asking myself, *Is this normal?* as if there is really some true measurement of what normalcy looks like. Please tell me you've done this too. I think all of us have probably looked at various family dynamics we've lived through and prayed, "God, help me to not repeat that cycle."

All I know for sure is that whatever it was that found its way into our bloodline manifested itself in my mother as sure as the innate beauty and vanity that were handed down. And I think that it's also just the very act of living that tends to stoke the fire of things that lie smoldering for a long time before you see them burst into the flames that can burn everything down. When I think about my childhood, it feels somewhat like a house on fire that I didn't even know I needed to escape from until years later when I realized it had the power to burn down everything new I was hoping to build.

CHAPTER 3

Why Would a Mother?

For years when our kids were little, Gulley—my best friend—and I used to take them to Santa's Wonderland during Thanksgiving break. "What is Santa's Wonderland?" you may be asking. Well, it's a money pit disguised as a magical North Pole substitute outside College Station, Texas, where you can take a hayride through an incredible display of Christmas lights and then later sit on Santa's lap and, if you're feeling extra adventurous, ride a mechanical bull. The movie *Urban Cowboy* has had a profound and lasting impact on Texas culture. As with all pop-culture touchstones, it should.

Anyhow, one year we were at Santa's Wonderland with the kids when a cold front blew through. This is winter in Texas. It'll be eighty-five degrees, and then five minutes later it's forty degrees and sleet is falling. We'd known this was a possibility, so we'd told the kids to bring jackets. But if you're a parent, you know that one of the most embarrassing things for a kid is if their friends see that they own a coat. It's mortifying. Owning a jacket is a societal reckoning that apparently you can't recover from if you're under eighteen years old.

So the kids ignored our advice, and we decided that this was a time to let the chips fall where they may. Sometimes the best teacher is the consequence of bad decisions. Gulley's son Will was about six years old and had been the strongest objector to wearing a jacket. But as the cold front blew in and the temperature continued to drop, Will turned to Gulley with an accusatory look in his big blue eyes and demanded, "Why would a mother not bring a jacket for her son?"

When I tell you that this sent Gulley and me into fits of laughter instead of sympathy, I am not lying. And it's become one of our trademark phrases anytime we're lamenting over how extra, overbearing, or neglectful our kids think we're being. "Why would a mother walk into the front office of the middle school?" "Why would a mother want to pack an extra sandwich in your lunch?" "Why would a mother tell you to go to bed when it's midnight and you're still watching TikToks?"

Mothers. The worst. Am I right?

There is an infinite number of things mothers do that our kids will never understand until . . . wait for it . . . they eventually have kids of their own and are also accused of not caring enough to make someone bring a jacket that they absolutely implored them to bring and were completely ignored. And there are also things some mothers do that legitimately beg the question "Why would a mother?"

In my early days of motherhood, after years of wrestling, I felt as though perhaps I could finally understand a little bit of my own mother. I'd had other epiphanies about her at different points in my life, but becoming a mother myself opened my eyes and my heart in a way that nothing else had up to that point. I didn't know how hard it was to endure sleepless nights or how lonely it could feel at times. I'd never known that level of being tired and all the emotions that go along with that. How can you look at your baby and love them so deeply yet long to escape back to a time when your biggest concern was getting home from dinner in time to watch the new episode of *Friends*? (Dear reader, there was a time called the pre-2000s, when we knew nothing of streaming services and were at the mercy of a VHS tape and our minimal ability to set something called a VCR to accurately record a show for us to watch later. It was stressful and fraught with the potential drama of accidentally recording over your wedding-reception video. Ask me how I know.)

All that to say, motherhood was significantly harder than I'd imagined it would be, and I began to feel as though maybe I was getting a glimpse into some of my own mother's battles and fragility. There were so many times when I started to understand that the answer to "Why would a mother?" was "Because she is doing the best she can."

* * * * * *

I'd love to use this moment to take you back to when it all began for me. The year 1969 was pivotal in American history. It was the summer of Woodstock, men landing on the moon, and Charles Manson. Also, Suzanne and Charles Marino got married. Charles (Marino, not Manson) and Suzanne were my parents, so obviously this was the event that had the most impact on my life. My parents didn't choose the hippie route that was such a part of American culture at that time but rather opted for the traditional college-to-job-to-marriage path that was preferred by parents everywhere and seemed to offer safety, stability, two kids, and a thirty-year mortgage.

I vividly remember certain things about my childhood. I can

feel the water of the sprinklers on my skin as I ran back and forth in the slick green grass with neighborhood kids. I can remember riding my bike to the pool, wearing just my swimsuit, flip-flops, and a towel wrapped jauntily around my neck. I can still picture the green shag carpet that was in our living room and remember how it felt under my feet. I recall simple summer days of playing giant games of freeze tag across every yard on our street with a roving gang of kids who ran in and out of one another's houses in search of Popsicles or someone else to join our group. I remember the day my eight-track tape player bled battery acid on my brand-new aqua-colored Gloria Vanderbilt jeans and ruined them. Has there ever been a tragedy so specific to 1979?

I remember what was by all measures a normal, uneventful childhood: a dad who worked long hours to provide a nice lifestyle, a mom who shooed my younger sister and me out the door in the mornings to make sure we got to the bus stop in time, and family dinners eaten around the table in our breakfast room. I think one of the beautiful things about childhood is that things must be terribly wrong for a kid to notice that something isn't right, and I was blissfully unaware of the faults that lay in my family's foundation, waiting to crack it wide open. But I also think part of me must have known something was off and was looking for a way to escape.

I could tell you stories about how as a five-year-old I would sneak out of the house early in the mornings and go knock on the neighbors' door and ask if I could play at their house. I used to make up elaborate tales that I would tell my grandparents about how I would ride my tricycle to U-Totem and buy candy for myself, and I guess I was convincing enough that they asked my mom if that was true. I have vague recollections of always feeling like I wanted to get away from my mom because I constantly had the sense that she wanted something from me that I couldn't give her—something that I wasn't meant to give her. (Incidentally, I once asked her after I had Caroline, "How did you know you were ready to have another baby?" She had my sister, Amy, four years after I was born. She replied, "Well, you were three and so independent. It made me want to have someone who needed me." *Well, I was three. How independent could I have been? Was I driving myself to preschool?*)

Because my family life seemed so normal to me, I didn't pay any more attention to it than to the air I breathed. I'll bet if you think back to your own life, you'll find it's difficult to remember much about the day-to-day of childhood, other than bits and pieces. But the memories that stand out are usually of either a really fun event or something that caused your whole world to shift.

The earthquake came for me when I was nine years old. I was about to walk two doors down to my best friend Caroline's house to spend the night, and I was eager to get there because we had big plans to play *Pong* and further dissect the relationship between Danny Zuko and Sandy Olsson from *Grease*. Perhaps later that night we would make our specialty, which was nacho-cheese Doritos covered in Cheez Whiz and then microwaved for thirty seconds. (Not one parent in the 1970s was ever concerned about things like gluten or artificial red dye or cheese in a jar that could survive on a shelf for upward of thirty years.)

My plans were thwarted when my mom informed me that she and my dad needed to talk to Amy and me before I left for my evening of fun and culinary delights. I remember sitting on the rust-colored floral couch in our family room as my mom said, "Your dad and I have decided that we need to be apart for a while, but nothing is really going to change. Your dad is moving into an apartment nearby, and it has a pool!" As if the pool was really going to be the thing to make it all a very exciting adventure.

If I'm completely honest with you, I don't remember even feeling sad about this. I knew that my parents were devastated as they told us, evidenced by their tears and quivering voices. I think there are few things more jarring to kids than when the adults in the room begin to cry. But my main memory of that night is my impatience to go spend the night with my friend. Maybe my desire to curl up in bunk beds and eat processed cheese was some sort of defense mechanism, but I think it's more likely that a nine-year-old who has never known any real discomfort doesn't have the emotional capacity or wisdom to comprehend the ripple effects that this one moment would have in her life over the course of the ensuing years.

Here's what I don't know for sure, because I'm the opposite of Oprah: Did my mom begin unraveling before the end of her marriage, or was the end of her marriage the beginning of the unraveling? Based on the pieces I've collected like some sort of archaeologist of emotional instability, I believe the unraveling started many years before but was carefully buried under layers of societal norms and traditional family routines and the presence of my dad, all combined to create a sense of stability that wasn't actually there. I wish I could look back at the earliest years of my life, before the divorce happened, and find signs that something was off. But the best I can do is tell you an anecdote that was told to me many times by my mom and seems to indicate that maybe I saw things I didn't even know were troublesome. She loved telling me that when I was a toddler, I'd occasionally walk into a room where she was and my brown eyes would flash darkly as I'd ask her, "What doin', Suzanne?"

Did I know something wasn't right? Because there were so many times over the course of my life that I'd ask some version of that same question.

· · · · · ·

After my parents' separation, the elementary school counselor was notified about the divorce. In what was maybe the worst inconvenience of all, I had to begin meeting once a week with her and a group of kids who were also dealing with various things so we could talk about our feelings. That was when I learned a truth about myself that stands to this day: I won't be coerced into talking about my feelings. I'm not interested in baring my soul or receiving the well-meaning sympathy of people who aren't in my inner circle. That is why I've never successfully lasted in a small group at church. I don't enjoy forced community. I realize this isn't how all small groups work, but it's my personal hill I will die on.

You know that feeling you get when all of a sudden it seems like everything you thought you knew begins to change? That's how I felt in that year after my parents' divorce. Everything felt shaky and uncertain. There were new land mines to constantly navigate, and my nine-year-old self quickly decided it was my job to try to keep everyone happy, which was a foolhardy mission at best. It resulted in behavior patterns where, for years, I tried to contort myself into what I thought people needed me to be, before I realized that wasn't great for my own emotional health. To this day, I sometimes have to stop myself from lying about something to make someone else feel better.

After the divorce, my mom got her real estate license and went back to work. This meant Amy and I came home from school to an empty house, where I was in charge since I was older. The specifics of that period are so foggy to me now because, well, many years have passed and my brain has chosen to instead remember all the lyrics to "Kiss on My List" by Hall and Oates. But I vividly remember feeling unmoored and off-balance.

Amy and I spent every other weekend with our dad. We'd pack our little rainbow duffel bags, and he would pick us up late Friday afternoon. I now realize that was the beginning of my awareness that I had to calculate what I chose to tell my mom, because after Dad dropped us back off on Sunday afternoons, she'd always ask, "Did you have a good time? Was it fun?" I quickly learned that if I answered yes, it would infuriate my mom or she would begin to cry, head to her bed, and stay there for days. Both reactions just made me feel guilty, so I learned to keep my mouth shut. I felt caught in the middle no matter what I did, and that was a lot to navigate as a fourth grader.

Late one night when Amy and I were staying with Dad, Mom was leaving the real estate office where she worked and a light fixture fell and hit her on the head. At the time, it didn't seem to be a big deal, but looking back now, I believe that injury was the genesis of what would become her lifelong struggle with prescription painkillers. We didn't know until years later just how much our mom self-medicated in various forms, but much of it started here. I think she found something that numbed not just her physical pain but also her mental state.

This was in the late 1970s, when you could go visit a doctor and get a truckload of Percocet. No one was really talking about addiction, and we had yet to watch VH1 *Behind the Music* specials about how drugs can ruin your life and cause your band to break up.

When my mom married my dad, she had converted to Catholicism. But now that they were divorced, the Catholic jig was up. We left Prince of Peace Catholic Church and somehow ended up attending a small charismatic Assemblies of God church called Northwest Tabernacle that met in a double-wide trailer. I feel like if your church has *tabernacle* in the name and meets in a trailer home, it makes a bold statement that says, "We aren't here to play around." While this whiplash church-culture move gave me a foundation for having a real relationship with Jesus, it also gave me some religious trauma, a forever side-eye about overly dramatic praise-and-worship dancing, and a tangible fear of potluck suppers due to some unfortunate gelatin salads I encountered.

In a way, the instant switch to this whole new religious experience stands as a monument separating the before and after of my childhood. Everything had felt very safe and secure at Prince of Peace. The rules were laid out clearly, and the rituals were very orderly and reverent. Suddenly I found myself in a new place both in life and in church that felt like the Wild, Wild West. Everything was lawless and chaotic. One minute you might be singing "Great Is Thy Faithfulness," and the next minute someone might be yelling out in tongues before passing out in the aisle of the trailer home. I was shook, as the kids say.

We'd scarcely had time to recover from this dramatic shift before another one came on its heels. My mom met a man who was ten years her junior and married him after a two-month courtship. She allowed him to move into the home where the mortgage was being faithfully paid by my dad every month, a place that once held the safety, joy, and innocence of my childhood. So, our house was also home to an interloper who had shown up to our first meeting, at Red Lobster of all places, with carnations wrapped in blue foil. Even as a kid, I knew that paltry floral display was a harbinger of less-than-optimal things to come. And I was correct.

A steady stream of men had come into and gone out of our lives since my dad moved out. They were all some version of the same person, and none of them seemed to come bearing any great intentions. But my mom existed in a world where she felt defined by her beauty and her ability to attract the opposite sex, and she excelled at both of those things. I'm not exactly sure why she decided to accept a marriage proposal less than a year after signing the divorce papers, but I wonder if it's because he was the first guy who asked. And I also have no doubt that she did it to lash out at my dad. Suzanne was a master at taking dramatic, sweeping actions that hurt her as much as, if not more than, anyone in her life. Nanny and Big Bob begged her not to go through with it. My sister and I cried and pleaded that she call it off. Even my dad tried to convince her it was a terrible idea on every level. She listened to exactly no one. The wedding took place in the living room of a family she'd met through the new church we attended.

Yes, it was as weird as it sounds.

I watched my mom, who was wearing a pale lavender velvet vest and skirt, walk through this family's entryway, past their set of La-Z-Boy recliners, to the fireplace, where the preacher

stood with the stranger who was about to become my stepfather. I may have been just ten years old, but I knew that no good
was going to come of it. After the wedding and a few sips of
punch, my mom and her new husband loaded my sister and me
into the car and dropped us off at my dad's house as they sped
off on their honeymoon. In the span of one year, I'd watched
everything I trusted fall apart. That day was the first time I
knew what devastation felt like.

A memory just came back to me while I was writing, and I
can't tell you how much I wish it had stayed repressed: Shortly
after they got married and he moved into our house, they hung
a sign on the door to the master bedroom that read, "Children,
stay away. There are adults at play."

It was like I was living in an X-rated Hobby Lobby.

Why would a mother?

CHAPTER 4

My First Mean Girl

The next four months were a blur of late nights and tears. More than once, I snuck downstairs to call my dad on the harvest-gold phone that hung in our kitchen. I'd beg him to come get me, realizing I had lost any version of the mom I once knew and had gained a pervading sense of helplessness to escape these strange new circumstances. I didn't want to be the kid at school with a new stepdad. I certainly didn't want to be told what to do by this strange man living in our house whose sole positive trait was his ability to make a good omelet. I'd transitioned from a carefree kid to feeling like it was my job to protect both my younger sister and my mom. I don't even know what I was protecting them from. I just had a general sense that this situation wasn't right, and my mom was acting more unhinged than I could ever remember.

There was a night during this time when a tornado hit our neighborhood in Houston. I'd always been afraid of the dark and dreaded nighttime. In fact, my mom once told me in all seriousness, "Maybe if you had been better about staying in bed at night, your dad and I would still be married," which feels like an appropriate thing to say to your elementary-aged child. I'll see your "things kids end up in counseling over" and raise you five hundred.

But that night was particularly terrifying, and our whole house shook as the storm intensified—a physical manifestation of all the turmoil inside those four walls. Lightning crashed, the power went out, and I wanted my mom. I wasn't allowed to just show up in her room (please remember that tasteless sign on the door), so I called out to her: "Mom! Come get me. I'm scared."

But she didn't come.

Maybe if I yelled louder. "Mama! Please come in my room! I'm really scared!"

Crickets.

As the wind howled around our house and the thunder boomed, I cried out again: "Mom! Please! Come! Get! Me!" She finally showed up, ordered me to go back to sleep, and abruptly left. She didn't care that I was terrified and wanted her to tell me it was going to be okay and the storm would pass. I felt abandoned and alone. Again. I was a kid who wanted her mom, and that was apparently no longer an option unless it was on her terms and her timetable.

The next morning, our street was strewn with large pine branches and debris from the storm, but the damage that had been done in my heart left no such outwardly visible trail.

That may explain my conversation a couple of weeks later. My stepdad was changing out the fluids in his truck in our driveway, and I saw a green liquid seeping out and asked him, "What is that?"

He replied, "It's antifreeze, but don't go near it. It's very poisonous."

And I looked him right in the eye and said, "I wish you'd drink it."

It wasn't long after that when my mom abruptly decided the marriage was over. I have no idea what this ultimatum looked like or even all the reasons, but I vividly remember feeling relieved as I watched my stepfather carry his bags out of the house. Maybe life would go back to what I'd known. Maybe I was going to be able to feel safe in my house again and not like I was constantly dodging quicksand. Back to the good old days when my biggest concern was whether that Friday night would be the time Sheriff Rosco P. Coltrane finally sent Bo and Luke Duke to the Hazzard County Jail for good. (This is a *Dukes of Hazzard* reference, for those of you too young to remember this Friday-night television staple.)

But a couple of days later, he showed up and began screaming at her from the driveway, "Suzanne! Come outside right now! Get out of the house and come talk to me!" as she sat on the couch and refused to move. All I could do was wonder what on earth our neighbors could possibly be thinking at this sordid new development on our quiet tree-lined suburban street. This is not who we had been. We had a mailbox that was a small replica of our house, for goodness' sake. My mom had been the PTO president just a year earlier. We were more respectable than having a mustachioed man in a bug-exterminator truck hollering at my mother from the driveway.

When he continued to yell and it became apparent he wasn't going to go quietly into the good night, my mom walked out our front door. My little sister was already in bed, so I sat there alone on our couch, biting my nails anxiously and wondering what I was supposed to do. There was no Girl Scout guide for how to de-escalate a domestic disturbance. Mercifully, our phone rang and one of our next-door neighbors was on the other end of the line: "Melanie? Are y'all okay? What is going on?"

I so clearly remember this moment of being seen by an adult—an actual adult paying attention to what was happening—and I burst into tears as I replied, "No! We are not okay. I'm so scared, and my mom is outside, and I don't know what's happening. Please help us!"

She remained calm as she said, "Don't worry, sweetie. It's going to be okay. Let me get off the phone, and you stay inside. I'll see you in a minute."

Relief ran through me with the realization that I was no longer in charge of this situation, and a few minutes later, the police showed up in front of our house, with sirens wailing and lights flashing. Somehow my simple childhood had devolved into an episode of *Cops*. I watched through our front window as the police handcuffed my stepfather, put him in the squad car, and drove away. My mom came inside, went straight to her bedroom, and shut the door without saying a word.

Our neighbor knocked softly on the front door, and after peeking through the peephole to ensure it was safe to answer, I opened the door and she asked, "Are you okay?"

Dear reader, I was not, in fact, okay. I hadn't been okay in months. But I nodded as she handed me a cookie she'd brought from her house. Then I went upstairs and tucked myself into bed, realizing then that so many of the hypothetical monsters I'd always been afraid of in the dark weren't the actual thing I needed to fear.

Not too long after that madness went down, my mom made

the decision to sell our house in Houston and move us to Beaumont, Texas, to live down the street from Nanny and Big Bob. You would think I might have been sad to move out of the home I'd grown up in, leave all my childhood friends, and live farther away from my dad, but the only thing I felt was relief that we were moving somewhere that seemed like it might be safe. And of all the things my mom did and however convoluted her reasons were for making the move, I will always be grateful for that decision because my grandparents proved to be an anchor we would all need for the years to come.

· · · · · ·

Suzanne was pure fun at times. She could make even the most mundane things feel like an adventure. A trip to Walmart was one of her life's delights, and she would let us load the cart with everything from new CoverGirl makeup to bunny slippers. When she was riding a high, she might decide to paint the kitchen at midnight and then take us to eat a Grand Slam breakfast at Denny's at two o'clock in the morning. It felt exhilarating. She could be delightfully scatterbrained and so random. One day she got into the car, looked down at the floorboard, and exclaimed, "Oh, look! A red hot!" as she popped a small red thing into her mouth, then quickly spit it out and said, "Oops! I think that was a Sudafed."

I asked her, "Either way, why would you pick something up off the floor of a car and eat it?" and we both laughed until we had tears running down our faces.

We would often spend the weekend at Nanny and Big Bob's lake house, and Mom was always up for floating in the lake with us and sitting on the dock while we fished for perch with our Snoopy fishing poles. For my thirteenth birthday, she let me invite a group of my friends to the lake house for the weekend, including a couple of my best friends from Houston. At the end of the weekend, we were so sad it was over and begged her to let us stay one more night. She made it happen and it felt like magic.

But at other times, she would break up with a boyfriend or start to romanticize what life with my dad had been like. She would create a narrative in her head about how she and my dad were going to get back together and then share that thought with Amy and me, which only caused us to never truly move past the divorce, because what kid doesn't want to believe her family will be back together? I guess reality would finally hit, and she would get in the bed and stay there for days. I never knew what was going to be her trigger, but I understood that any peace or joy was going to be short-lived and that I should never let my guard down.

Have you ever had a relationship that contained multitudes of feelings and meanings, depending on the situation? And have you spent time trying to figure out the other person because you can't reduce them to just one truth? My mom was both light and dark in my life. As a child, I didn't know about things like borderline personality disorder and bipolar mood swings. I didn't realize she took a handful of pills that kept her up and then brought her crashing down. Walking into my house after school often felt like I was on a potentially treacherous game show where I had no idea what I would find behind curtain number two.

I remember coming home from summer camp one time, and Suzanne had completely redecorated my room using as inspiration the pink-and-green Laura Ashley comforter set I'd been dying for. It was fantastic. She'd painted the walls a light pink and then feather-dusted over that with white paint to create a textured effect. There was nothing any woman in my family loved more in the 1980s than some sort of decorative wall treatment, and that was her masterpiece. But then a couple of days after the room reveal, she blew up at me and told me I hadn't appreciated what she'd done. She threatened to take it all back. I was stunned. I thought I'd acted very excited, since *I was very excited,* but somewhere my reaction fell short of her expectations. So I spent my years at home walking a delicate balance of trying to be myself while also constantly trying to gauge who she wanted me to be.

Here's a question maybe you've also asked yourself over the years: How does one look at their childhood objectively? There are so many inner workings that are hidden, and that was perhaps never truer than in the 1970s and '80s. So many baby boomers raised their kids in much the same way they were raised, where any feelings and opinions their kids had were largely inconsequential. As children of this era, some of us were just collateral damage on our parents' journeys to finding their own happiness and, frankly, just lucky to be there rolling around without seatbelts in the back of a wood-paneled station wagon, inhaling secondhand cigarette smoke. "Put on this mask with eyeholes you can barely see out of, and use this plastic pumpkin to go collect candy from strangers. It's all fine."

And I do feel as though the pendulum has probably now swung too far the other way. I see young parents today on a constant quest to make every part of childhood magical and wonderful for their kids. I want to pull them aside and say,

"Look, Kayleigh, the concept of the tooth fairy is magical enough without you scattering glitter all over your child's bedroom." We are giving these children upward of one American dollar for a used tooth that hardly knew a toothbrush whilst it was still in its owner's mouth. Maybe we all need to settle down and get off Pinterest and quit buying what the Instagram influencers are selling about how you get only eighteen summers with your kids (as dramatic music plays in the background of a reel). None of us are meant to live with that kind of pressure to make every second count. Some seconds are boring and monotonous, and you can just be thankful that a particular day when the dog threw up and your kid forgot their lunch and you fought with your husband is over and done. But back to the story . . .

Our move to Beaumont coincided with my middle school years, and you know what everyone says: Middle school really is the best time of your life. Everyone is so secure and supportive, and there's no drama or angst. But not really. Truthfully, at least for a while, the move seemed to be the best thing for all of us. I think living down the street from her parents gave my mom some of the stability and accountability she needed, and it gave Amy and me a safe haven.

Walking down the street to Nanny and Big Bob's house always felt like a delicious escape to what I knew intuitively home should feel like. Nanny was always willing to stop whatever she was doing to listen to my stories about whatever had happened at school that day while she made my very favorite snack, a chili-cheese sandwich. (This was a toasted sandwich with canned chili and melted cheese, preferably served with a side of nacho-cheese Doritos. And, yes, it was as delicious as it sounds.)

I spent almost as many nights at Nanny's house as I did at home. She'd make homemade banana pudding, and we'd stay up late to watch Johnny Carson on *The Tonight Show*. On the weekends, Nanny and Big Bob often took us to the lake house. We'd jump off the dock and swim until we were exhausted and sun-soaked during the day and then play multiple rounds of Skip-Bo at night.

Our move to Beaumont also brought us to a church I loved. The youth group at Cathedral in the Pines became a sanctuary. I'll be honest and tell you I don't know how much was about Jesus and how much was about all the fun girls and cute boys in the group, but it was the first time I actually *wanted* to go to church. I mean, it still had its share of church-culture oddities because it was the 1980s, but it was full of love and warmth and the best of intentions, even if it did instill a little fear in me about the Rapture happening and the possibility that I might be left behind.

Meanwhile, my mom had started dating again, but this time it was a guy we really liked. John was a bachelor with no kids of his own, but he seemed to enjoy being around Amy and me and was always willing to play a few rounds of Trivial Pursuit or Spades. He'd often cook dinner for all of us, and I even remember one day when he picked me up from school when I was sick and the nurse couldn't find my mom. John helped me get into the house, warmed up some soup, and turned on *Days of Our Lives* for me while I lay on the couch. I was grateful for his presence in our lives. He made my mom happier and lighter than she had been in years. Amy and I always wanted him around because he made everything seem more fun.

But then they broke up for the first time.

I say "the first time" because the next six years were full of almost constant upheaval as my mom and John broke up and got back together over and over again. I guess they were like that old saying "Can't live together, can't live apart." Their dynamic reminded me of one of my favorite shows during my teen years, *Cheers*. I watched the reruns every night before bed, and the truth was, I had my own Sam-and-Diane situation playing out in my house but a lot less funny or endearing. And my mom took no prisoners during the breakups. Once when I was in ninth grade, I made the mistake of telling her that I really missed John and wished they would get back together. She looked right at me and said, "Why? He doesn't even really like you and thinks you and Amy are both spoiled brats."

Then they got back together, but I was left with all the questions about how he really felt about us—and if he did feel the way she said he did, why would my mom stay with him?

And then another breakup came. This one was *supposedly* for good, which I guess is why my mom tearfully called us into the kitchen one night and asked that we bring all the various gifts he'd given us over the years. Amy and I walked into our kitchen—ironically decorated with cheery, hat-wearing geese stenciled on the walls—with a handful of trinkets he'd given us, and Mom announced, "We need to burn all these things. I don't want any reminders of him in our lives."

This kind of back-and-forth went on for years and became a blueprint for what I thought must just be a normal relationship dynamic. It's hard to know how unhealthy something is when you're living right in the middle of it and often being told you're the problem. You just assume, like Taylor Swift, *Hi, I'm the problem. It's me.*[1]

I was a sophomore in high school when my heart got broken for the first time. I'd cheated on my boyfriend with another guy and then was devastated when my boyfriend found out and, understandably, broke up with me. Were Mom's unhealthy relationship dynamics imprinted on me? Was I following her path? Nevertheless, my heart was broken over my poor choices and losing a boy I'd really cared about. I spent a lot of time crying in my bedroom with my *Chicago 17* cassette on repeat.

A few days of this passed before Mom knocked on my door and asked if we could talk. I thought that maybe she wanted to help me process this first heartbreak, but she walked through the door of my room, sat down on my bed, and started to cry as she announced, "John and I have broken up, and this time it's for good." There was no space for my feelings or struggles, and as you can imagine, I felt more alone after she left my room than I had before she came in. She was always the thermostat that controlled the temperature.

My mom and I spent my high school years locked in a tedious, exhausting dance of competition, envy, love, anger, laughter, and tears. Neither of us knew how to be what the other needed. I was too independent, headstrong, and willing to call out the hypocrisy I saw in what she expected from me versus what I saw her living out. I worked hard to keep her volatile mood swings at bay and then resented her for it. I wanted her to be proud of me or maybe just really see me, but it seemed like she was always too wrapped up in her own search for significance to pay much attention to mine.

My mom was my first mean girl.

She was quick to let me know where I wasn't good enough and used criticism or silence to tear down anything I built. She could destroy me with a couple of well-timed words that felt specifically curated to hit me in the most tender places. There were times she raged at everything and everyone in her path. The words and accusations that came out of her mouth were legendary. I never knew when she was going to turn on me for what felt like no reason at all. I rarely felt any sense of safety or peace around her, and the little there was could evaporate at any moment. She had a way of twisting my words and actions to ensure that everything was always my fault. But then she had this way of sometimes seeming so childlike and helpless, which caused me to feel protective of her. As much as she could hurt me, I never wanted to hurt her back. Our dynamic was something along the lines of "I hate you—please don't leave me."

When I think of her now, it's of someone who was always in search of a peace she couldn't find, and it makes me sad. I spent my childhood and much of my adulthood watching her throw away any chance she had at happiness. And her lack of those things caused her to resent any that I found. Suzanne was the only person who ever looked at me and said, "You're such a disappointment."

She had a way of saying something that felt like it might be a compliment but had a hidden undertone: "You're almost as pretty as your new blond friend." Sometimes she apologized later and said she hadn't meant it, but there isn't really any way hateful words from the person who is supposed to love you the most—the person who should feel like your safest place—aren't going to leave a mark and amplify dormant insecurities.

That wounded me deeply, and I ceased to trust anyone or anything. The fact that many of her accusations toward me were couched in religious guilt managed to convince me that God viewed me as one of His great disappointments. The number of times I walked down an aisle at church or some sort of church camp to beg God to forgive me for being such a failure would cause even Billy Graham to say, "Girl, I think you're good."

. . . . . .

If you're wondering where my dad was in all this, he was there. He never failed to show up for his appointed weekends with my sister and me. He called me on the phone every single night of my life to check in until I was out of college. He was never absent, not even for a day. But my mother had done her best to diminish him in our eyes because my close relationship with my dad was at the top of her list of all the things she resented about me. He had found happiness with a woman who would ultimately become our stepmom, and in Suzanne's eyes, that was probably the worst transgression of all.

Amy and I liked his new girlfriend because she made the weekends we spent at his house more fun in a way that only a woman can. We had picnics and went shopping, and later on, she patiently taught me how to drive a stick shift in her new Porsche. Let's all have a moment of reverence for any woman who would let a fifteen-year-old girl still figuring out the difference between the clutch and the brake get behind the wheel of her Porsche. This alone should qualify someone for sainthood.

The more Suzanne saw my dad creating a happy new life for himself, the more she resented it—and the more she tried to paint him as an absentee dad who had abandoned us.

All her accusations caused me to build up anger and resentment toward my dad and stepmom to the point that, during my sophomore year of high school, when my dad called to tell me they'd gotten married, I informed him I never wanted to speak to him again. I'd spent most of my childhood believing my dad to be my greatest hero, but my mom had inserted a dark cloud in that narrative and done her best to make me question everything about him with no regard for how this would affect me.

I don't know that there is much that's more damaging to a young girl than for someone to make her believe that her father might not really love her, especially when it's not the truth.

Dads are the lenses that young girls see themselves through, and Suzanne's accusations about him chipped away at both the hero my dad had always been to me and my own sense of self. I knew I was a lot like my dad, so I felt that my mom viewed my dad and me as a terribly flawed, godless duo who deserved any bad thing that came our way.

I never shared with my dad any of the things my mom said about him during those years, because I knew it would make him feel bad. Eventually, Dad and I would mend the rift she caused, but there were always lingering questions and doubts in my mind. I felt a loyalty to Suzanne that's hard to explain, but I think it was partly because she always cast herself in the role of victim and I bought it. I felt bad for her even as I resented her for doing that. Not to mention that I was always afraid to ask my dad about her accusations, because what if they turned out to be true? That felt like a potential heartbreak I couldn't handle, as it would mean either my dad wasn't what I thought he was or my mom was a liar. Neither of those was an outcome I wanted to process during my teen years. It felt like my job was to hold all the pieces of my life together and try to make everyone happy—and, most of all, to keep Suzanne from spinning out.

There are intangible, nurturing assurances a girl needs in her life that should come from a mother's practically unconditional love and support.

And what I mostly felt from my mom was simmering resentment.

. . . . . .

Have you ever thought that if people really knew you, they probably wouldn't like you? That if you showed anyone your true self, you might scare them straight? That's how I spent most of my high school years. I fully believed that no one would really love me if they knew the real me. I let people see only the parts of me that seemed most palatable, working hard to make myself infinitely likable and charming.

I think as humans we tend to sabotage anything we think we don't deserve. This explains why I picked up a habit of destroying relationships as a defense mechanism. I would hurt someone before they could hurt me. Most of all, I lived for the drama of falling in love and then falling out of love in equally chaotic fashion. I was searching desperately for someone to love me for me, but I was nowhere near secure enough to let anyone in. I didn't know what a healthy relationship should look like, so I spent a lot of time creating needless drama and ruining almost anything that was good.

I saw other girls as my competition, especially the ones I deemed prettier or smarter. When I was a freshman in high school, I invited my friend Julie to join me at church youth group for a lock-in. She had a great time and confessed to me the next day that she had a crush on a guy in the group named Kevin. I'd never paid much attention to Kevin, but as soon as Julie deemed him crush-worthy, I decided I'd go after him for myself. And I did that all in a manipulative, backhanded way where I acted like I was talking to him about her when really I was planting the seeds for him to like me instead. Then, when my plan worked, I dumped him, because it was never about me really liking him.

Instead of admiring what made other girls around me strong or brave, I often tore them down both in my mind and to others. I was a broken girl who didn't have the first clue I even needed to be healed. I just thought that was what life looked like and the way people operated. I developed the patterns I'd seen played out by my mom. I blame her and too many of episodes of *Dallas* for this. I'd become a mean girl.

I followed my mom's route and found temporary security and purpose in whatever guy I happened to be dating at the time and had a gift of completely transforming myself into whom and what I thought he wanted me to be. The fact that I viewed Bud and Sissy from *Urban Cowboy* as the ideal relationship is indicative of my understanding of what a healthy relationship should be.

During my junior year of high school, I started dating Andy. He was a year older than me and had a reputation as kind of a bad boy, which *yes, please.* He drove a black sports car and bought me a six-pack of Bartles & Jaymes berry wine coolers for our first date, and that was the first time I ever got drunk. It was fantastic. Just like that, all my inhibitions were gone. I didn't worry about what anyone thought of me. Alcohol was everything I didn't know I'd been looking for in life. That was the beginning of it being my emotional crutch for years. After our first date, Andy and I were inseparable except for when we weren't because we would have these huge, dramatic fights. My friends all hated him, which only served my belief that we were like a modern-day Romeo and Juliet and no one understood the depth of our love. I'd become my mother.

Andy and I dated on and off for the rest of my high school years. He became my everything, and I didn't realize all the ways he constantly tore me down, because it was all I knew. In an odd way, it felt comforting and familiar. That is what I thought love looked like. He would lash out at me because he thought I'd paid too much attention to someone else, but then he would do something special—like when he bought extravagant gifts for me for the twelve days leading up to Christmas just like in the song. Let's all give thanks that he didn't give me three French hens, because I have never cared for a bird.

By the end of my senior year, I was isolated from all my girlfriends. I had made Andy my entire world and felt as though I couldn't live without him. He represented stability to me, and it was amazing to feel like I was the center of someone's universe. I decided my friends were just jealous of our incredible connection. Andy was my escape from home. My mom didn't like him and he didn't like her, probably because they were basically the same person.

The night of my high school graduation, Andy was going to pick me up and drive me to the ceremony. But first I had to be part of a photo session in my living room. My mom had gone back to college to earn her degree, and my sister was graduating from eighth grade. That meant we all had to pose for pictures in our caps and gowns together. And it was made clear that my mom's accomplishment was the most important of the evening even though her actual graduation ceremony had happened two weeks earlier and I thought this was going to be my night. By the time Andy picked me up, I was beyond annoyed and had never felt more like I wanted to escape all the insanity. We talked about the possibility of running off and getting married. Thank you, baby Jesus, that even though I was only seventeen, some good sense prevailed.

I lied to my parents and said I was going to Crystal Beach with some girlfriends for the week after graduation. In reality, Andy and I went to the beach and spent the entire time together planning our future. I was looking for an escape from Suzanne, and he was there. After that week, I decided that I wouldn't leave Andy and thus wouldn't attend Texas A&M in the fall like I'd planned, but I wasn't sure how to break the news to my parents. That university had been my dream for as long as I could remember, but I was willing to throw it all away for "true love." I went ahead and attended orientation that summer. Then exactly two weeks before I was supposed to move into the dorm, I went to Fish Camp, which is essentially a fun summer-camp-type experience for incoming freshmen to indoctrinate them into all things Aggie. Those three days at Fish Camp shifted something inside me. I met so many new people and, all of a sudden, couldn't wait to go to Texas A&M even if it meant breaking up with Andy. So I called him on a pay phone the last night of Fish Camp and broke up with him.

Let's process two things here:

1. A pay phone. This was a staple of Gen X life that required either plenty of quarters or someone who would accept a collect call. How did we live that way?
2. I broke up with my boyfriend of two years over the phone.

It's like I got a glimpse of what life could be if I could just leave behind everything I knew, and it stirred something I'd buried deep inside.

However, Andy was waiting for me when I returned home, and he vowed that we'd make it work even though we'd be at different schools in different cities. I resisted for a while, but once I stepped onto the Texas A&M campus and felt completely overwhelmed in that way you do when you're a freshman in college in a new city surrounded by new people, I acquiesced and we got back together. I ended up transferring to Stephen F. Austin, where he was, for the spring semester—a move that only served to increase the toxic nature of our relationship to an abusive point. I started to recognize a bad pattern playing out that had been handed down from my mom, and I knew it wasn't okay. My fall semester at A&M had shown me enough of what life could be, and I wanted more of that, even though I was terrified to let go of all I knew and grab hold of it. But that's exactly what I did.

I informed my dad that I wanted to transfer back to A&M, and he made all the phone calls and helped me file the paperwork to make that happen. That summer after my freshman year, I finally broke up with Andy for good. My mom had moved to Oklahoma by that time, so I spent the summer wrapped in the security of living with Me-Ma and Pa-Pa. These were my dad's parents, and I was their oldest grandchild. If you have ever felt like you needed a safe place to land during a hard time, then you might understand what a crucial role that season played in my life. Me-Ma and Pa-Pa adored me in that unconditional way only grandparents can and gave me so much stability and security. They built me up in ways I didn't even recognize or know I needed, but I believe they ultimately gave me the strength to make some good choices for the first time ever. They saw something in me that I didn't see in myself, and I desperately wanted to live up to that.

• • • • • •

I went back to Texas A&M for my sophomore year of college, and while it's a stretch to say I was making great decisions, I was moving forward. But the summer after my sophomore year, I felt homesick for life with my mom and sister. The three of us had lived together all those years in some dysfunctional version of *Gilmore Girls*, and part of me wanted to go back to that place that at least felt familiar as I landed on the precipice of real adulthood, so I did. At that time, Amy was living with my mother in Oklahoma. Mom had been offered a great job there and decided she needed a fresh start. She seemed settled and at peace. And I'll always remember that summer as a happy time of taking late-night trips to Walmart and watching movies together curled up on the couch. It was great until a new guy showed up.

He drove a Corvette. He wore a white suit. He didn't care at all about my sister and me. In fact, he initially broke up with my mom because he wasn't interested in marrying someone with kids—a fact she tearfully shared with Amy and me as if that were somehow our fault. But they got back together, and suddenly, for the second time in my life, I begged my mom not to get married to someone she'd known for only a couple of months. By that time, I was old enough to see the pattern she had of creating chaos right as she found some stability. She had a great job she loved, she was making good money, and she and

Amy had a nice life in Oklahoma. Yet now she was ready to sabotage it all for a man she barely knew.

I went back to College Station for my junior year of college, praying my mom wouldn't go through with the marriage, which was tentatively planned for November. And one night right in the middle of Aggie football season (still my favorite season of the year), she called and asked if she could come visit me for the weekend. This had never happened even once since I'd been at college, so I happily told her that I would love for her to come and that maybe we could even go to a football game.

That Friday afternoon, I picked her up at the little airport in College Station, and as we were headed back to my apartment, she said, "Well, I guess I need to tell you that John is heading here to see me this weekend to try to talk me out of getting married." In case you've forgotten, John was her boyfriend during my high school years. And here's the truth: I was excited to see John (the only one of her old flames I liked) but also felt that familiar pain of disillusionment as I realized the weekend visit wasn't at all about her coming to see me; it was merely a way for her to get away from her fiancé to see an ex-boyfriend without causing any suspicions. Once again, I became the keeper of the secrets my mom kept from everyone else in her life, also knowing I had the power to blow it all up if I wanted to. That's a weird line for a twenty-year-old to walk. And here's the thing: I didn't want to wreck her life, because it usually felt like she was doing a pretty good job of that by herself. Besides, something in me still wanted her approval and felt protective toward her. I thought her spending time with John might be what she needed to be able to make a good decision and find real happiness.

She spent most of that weekend with John, and I was just her relationship mule. I can tell you that I have no idea what happened between them that weekend or who wouldn't agree to marry whom or all the reasons it didn't work out. I just know that when I dropped my mom off at the airport, she was in tears and seemed like a lost little girl, one who needed so much more than anyone could give her. So, when I found myself wearing a terrible teal-colored satin dress as I served as a bridesmaid in her wedding to the new guy a few weeks later, I knew that a shift had occurred.

A few months afterward, I flew to Oklahoma to visit my mom for the weekend. I wanted to see her and Amy, even if I wasn't thrilled about the part where I was going to have to stay at my new stepdad's house, where she and Amy had moved after the wedding. Suzanne picked me up at the airport and suggested we go grab a bite to eat.

As the waitress was setting our drinks down in front of us, I said, "I can't wait to see Schotzie and Soxy! I've missed them," referring to the two cats we'd had since I was in second grade.

My mom focused on squeezing the lemon into her ice tea as she said, "Well, I've been meaning to tell you something about that. James decided he didn't like the cats, so I had to get rid of them. I put an ad in the classifieds that advertised two sweet elderly long-haired cats free to a good home, and a nice family came and adopted them."

She gave away my fourteen-year-old cats.

And let's be clear: Telling your almost-adult child that you "put an ad in the classifieds" is the equivalent of telling a kid their dog "went to live on a nice farm where he could chase rabbits all day" when it had actually died. Lies.

I was absolutely stunned. It was one of those moments when you realize you didn't think something could be worse and then it 100 percent got worse.

The cats incident felt like a tangible symbol of all the ways, over the course of my childhood, that my mother repeatedly didn't choose me. She didn't even give me the option to come get the cats, which I totally would have done if given the choice. In that moment, all I wanted was to walk out of that restaurant, get on a plane, and never look back.

Instead, I looked at her and said, "Well, James doesn't like Amy and me either. Are you going to put a classified ad in the paper to get rid of us? Two beautiful long-haired brunettes. Free to a good home."

"Well, now you're just being ridiculous and overdramatic," she said with a wave of her hand as she kept stirring her ice tea. Back then, I didn't know about gaslighting, but now I do. If you have someone in your life who consistently manages to shift the blame to you or discounts your feelings, then you understand what it feels like.

I hardly ever went home after that. I wasn't even sure where or what home looked like. I vividly remember the pain of the realization that, as much as I'd wanted things to be different, home was most definitely not with my mother.

CHAPTER 5

The Truth of It All

I'm currently on a writing retreat in the mountains of North Carolina with my friends Sophie and Erin. It's something I've always wanted to do, largely because I've longed to say things like "I wrote this book while looking out at the mountains from the front porch of a remote cabin nestled in the pines . . . ," which is decidedly more glamorous than the writing experience with my first several books: "I wrote this book as I smelled the burnt cheese from someone's bacon-gouda sandwich while I sat in a dirty faux-leather chair at my neighborhood Starbucks." So, when Sophie and Erin invited me to join them for a five-day writing extravaganza in the mountains, I accepted without hesitation. I also hoped it would provide a much-needed jump start to my writing process, which up until now had looked a lot like deciding the oscillating fan in my bedroom needed to be cleaned before I could possibly concentrate on writing the book I was now legally bound to write. I am a legendary procrastinator and have convinced myself, if not my loved ones, that it is part of my charm.

We were at dinner one night after a day of writing and discussing our various chapters and topics, when Erin asked me, "What was the beginning of your knowing you needed to heal from your relationship with your mom? When did you know you were damaged?" That line of questioning was yet another reason I've benefited from this writing retreat, because not one time has a barista at Starbucks asked me thought-provoking questions that help me tell a story.

So let me tell you what I told Erin and Sophie over a plate of loaded Tater Tots at the Ugly Dog Public House in Highlands, North Carolina. Three things happened in my late teens and early twenties that proved to be significant for me in ways I can really see only when I look back now.

It all began when I met my best friend, Gulley, during my sophomore year of college. Not only have I mentioned her in chapters 2 and 3, but I have also written an entire book about my friendship with her, called *Nobody's Cuter than You*. But I'm going to tell the pivotal part of that story again here, assuming you either haven't read that book or at least haven't committed it to memory. Gulley and I met when we both became Diamond Darlings for the Texas A&M baseball team. That means we were essentially hostesses for the baseball team and did everything from serving as bat girls to handing out programs to taking potential recruits on campus tours, all while wearing enormous bows in our permed hair because this was the early 1990s. Today's Diamond Darlings have to wear batting helmets at all times, which we find to be a tragic development, even though it probably does make sense from a safety standpoint.

At any rate, we spent many baseball weekends road-tripping to all the away games, because this was back in the days of the

Southwest Conference and all our opponents were in the state of Texas. One of the trips was to Fort Worth to watch the Aggies play Texas Christian University (TCU). A whole group of us were spending the weekend at our friend Jen's house because she was from Dallas, and when we arrived, we realized there weren't enough beds for everyone. For some reason that is still a mystery to me, I volunteered to share a twin bed with Gulley. And here's what you need to know about me: I don't enjoy sharing a bed with anyone. I'm a high-maintenance sleeper who requires more pillows than I want to admit publicly, a fan set at just the right speed for both ambient noise and airflow, and room to move about the mattress. But I jumped in that bed with Gulley, and we spent the entire night talking about our childhoods, our friendships, our ex-boyfriends, and the ways we had been hurt in the past.

We discovered that night that we had a shared experience of a damaged parent who hadn't been capable of loving us, and we talked about all the ways that continued to affect the way we saw ourselves. Gulley was the first person I ever opened up to about my whole, real, damaged self. Suddenly I didn't feel so alone. God had brought someone into my life who totally understood me and where I'd come from, and I knew I'd found a soft place to land. If you've ever had that experience, then you know this seems like some sort of small miracle—that moment when you realize you're not the only one who's been through some hard things.

Realizing that someone really got me made me feel secure enough to begin to examine the things from my childhood that I'd stuffed down deep, trying to Scarlett O'Hara that business with the old "I'll think about it tomorrow."[1] It was one of those moments when I could see the hand of God so clearly putting a piece of me back together through a person I didn't even know I was looking for until she showed up. So it was in the spring of 1991 that I knew Gulley and I would always protect each other at all costs.

That was stage one of my healing: finding someone who related to what I'd been through and loved me for exactly who I was, flaws and all. Oh, but wait. There's more.

About a year later, while I was still at A&M, my friend Jen basically dragged me to a Bible study called Breakaway. I was coming off a series of unfortunate choices, including a broken engagement, as I unwittingly lived out so many of the generational mistakes my mother had carved out years before. Jen knew that I was searching for answers and that I'd reached a place that felt raw with longing as I looked for hope and redemption. I'd grown up in the church. I'd asked Jesus into my heart way back in elementary school. I'd spent multiple summers at various Vacation Bible Schools, singing songs and making crafts with Popsicle sticks. I knew all the words and movements to "Father Abraham," for goodness' sake. I'd been actively involved in my high school youth group and cried salty tears around a bonfire as a cute boy with a guitar played his rendition of "Friends" by Michael W. Smith.

But I hadn't grown up in a church tradition that gave much grace for mistakes. That, compounded with a mom who wasn't afraid to heap a healthy portion of guilt and shame on me, had caused me to become a nominal Christian at best. Could Jesus love a girl who enjoyed drinking Boone's Farm Strawberry Hill wine straight out of the bottle? Was there forgiveness for all the ways I'd failed over and over again? Was there grace for the years I'd spent running directly away from God and trying just about everything I could find to make myself feel better?

As it turns out, yes to all the above.

Breakaway was a huge turning point. I was surrounded by people my age who were passionate about Jesus and, more important, talked specifically about His love, mercy, and endless compassion. I had lived most of my life in a theological place that most resembled "Sinners in the Hands of an Angry God" and had finally come to a place where people talked about a Jesus who was bigger than my baggage and moral failings. A Jesus who wasn't even one bit afraid of my mess. A Jesus who wanted to use those very things I'd gotten wrong as powerful parts of my story. It turns out that I didn't have to work hard to make Him love me; He just did. He just loved me, all of me. And He wasn't scared of the darkest parts of myself, which I'd always felt I had to hide and had caused me to run far away before I could be cast out like Hester Prynne with a scarlet *A* on my chest. (Note that my big takeaway when I read *The Scarlet Letter* during my junior year of high school was that it felt eerily similar to my church youth group. I find that both disturbing and kind of funny in retrospect.)

So much of my religious baggage had been tied up in the hypocrisy I'd seen in my house and in the church, but what I realized as I began examining faith on my own was that Jesus is the thing that holds fast despite human failings. I get the whole current trend of everyone trying to deconstruct their faith, but in a way, I think we're making it more complicated than it needs to be.

Faith is not a riddle to be solved but rather a journey our hearts are on, and God isn't afraid of our questions or our doubts. Ask away, my friend. I've found that the questions I've asked have only made my faith grow. Don't let the way other humans have let you down—or the ways you've let yourself down—cloud the goodness of who God can be in your life. We are people who wanted to create New Coke when there was a perfectly good Coca-Cola already. People are going to screw up a good thing approximately 100 percent of the time in our delightful tendency to believe we can make anything better, so the church placed in our hands is going to look a little messy. We've gotten it very wrong at times and will continue to do so. But Jesus is good and true and bigger than any of our minds will ever be able to fathom, and I think He's more than okay with the doubts we wrestle with until we come to that realization. But back to the topic at hand.

Breakaway Ministries and letting it sink deep into my marrow that Jesus didn't view me as a huge disappointment beyond redemption was stage two of my healing process. The way Jesus came in and rewired the deepest parts of my trauma and insecurity is still the cornerstone of my life.

As for stage three, let me tell you about Perry Shankle. I graduated from Texas A&M in the spring of 1994 and moved to San Antonio. That is where I found a company willing to hire a speech communications major who had graduated with an illustrious 2.0 GPA. I don't mean to brag about my academic prowess; it's just part of who I am. A gentlewoman and a scholar.

Perry and I met through Breakaway about a month before I graduated, but our friend Gregg connected us again after he learned we were both in San Antonio. Perry had moved back home to finish up school, and I was now a career woman. I feel like "career woman" should be in quotation marks because, despite my array of suits from Casual Corner and slingback pumps from Payless ShoeSource, I really had no idea what I was doing in my job helping people invest their retirement money. I apologize if I helped you at any point with your investment portfolio and beg that you immediately go in search of better financial advice.

After about six months of friendship, Perry and I discovered that what we had was perhaps more than just being good friends. I'd realized this about three months in but spent the following three months waiting on him to catch up and get the memo that we had a love connection. Once that finally occurred, we knew quickly that we would end up getting married. So, in what is a traditional move before committing one's life to someone else, it was time to introduce Perry to my parents. I'd told him the basic overarching story of my childhood and the various traumas contained therein, but it was time for him to meet the starring players. And it's an interesting thing when you bring a fresh set of eyes into a dynamic that's as familiar to you as the cowlick that prevents you from having bangs that look like Reese Witherspoon's.

Perry and I ended up flying to Oklahoma so he could meet my mom. I hadn't really forgiven her for what she'd done to the cats, but it still felt important that she meet Perry. Of course, James was there, too, but I really didn't want to think about that awkward aspect of the visit. It turned out to be fairly uneventful, except for Sunday morning when Perry accidentally walked in on James curling his hair with a curling iron in the bathroom. I wish I were lying about this, but it's burned into my memory (no pun intended), and I can't know it alone.

Then a few weeks later, my dad and stepmom, Cherrie, came

to San Antonio and we all went to eat Mexican food because that's what you do when you visit San Antonio. After that initial meeting, Perry said that he didn't believe the terrible things my mom had told me about them over the years. She'd spent years planting toxic seeds of all the ways my dad had abandoned us and how Cherrie was complicit in all of it.

As we sat on the couch in my apartment that night, Perry, in his trademark up-front and honest way, gently said, "What you've been told doesn't add up with the people I met. A dad who abandons his family doesn't call that family every single night to check in with them." I knew in that moment that he was right, because he'd just said the thing out loud that I'd been trying to reconcile in my mind for years. It seemed accurate and had long been something I felt to be true, but I hadn't wanted to examine it too closely because of what that would mean about my mom. Had my mom willingly created a narrative that caused so much emotional damage and hurt in me?

Soon after, I told my mom that I felt like I had some healing to do regarding her divorce from my dad. I informed her that I was going to sit down with my dad and ask him what happened all those years ago from his perspective. I wanted to know why he left—what exactly went wrong. It felt like there had to have been a catalyst for it all.

And that's when, in a moment of pure honesty that confounds me to this day, Suzanne looked at me and said, "Well, what I told you may not have been the whole story." She then went on to tell me the truth about everything that caused the wreckage of their marriage. She was the one who had cheated multiple times. She was the one who had asked for the divorce. Essentially everything she had accused my dad of over the years was something she had been the one to commit.

As the words came from her mouth, years of lies and half truths unfolded before me, and I realized that the narrative she'd let us live out hadn't been true at all. In her need to vilify my dad, she didn't care that Amy and I were the collateral damage. It didn't matter that her deceit caused so much pain in my life, because her need to be the victim was more important than protecting her children.

Please note that she didn't ever apologize for lying in the first place. Even years later when I reminded her that she'd confessed the reality of the situation to me and I wasn't letting her act like a victim anymore, her response was "I should've never told you the truth."

Yes, the truth-telling was the real problem.

When I talked to my dad a week later about all that my mom had finally confessed, he nodded as he listened to me. He knew that had been the case, although maybe not to the full extent, but he hadn't wanted to create a "he said, she said" situation that would only cause more hurt and confusion. I learned so much that day from my dad about what it means to take the high road, to know that the truth will prevail, and to do your best to protect your child where you can. Sometimes there isn't anything to gain by engaging with words, but there can be so much power in your actions. Show up, do the right thing, love with your whole heart, and sacrifice your own need to defend yourself when you know that the truth will eventually come to light on its own. It's not that he did things perfectly so much as he did them honorably and with integrity.

This pivotal season was stage three of my healing journey. The thing Perry brought to me was perspective. He was able to see my life through a different lens, which gave him a clarity I'd never had.

But let me just clarify that this was stage three of what has been more like a ten-stage process that I'm often still trying to reconcile. There was so much more to come, because, as you are probably aware, life always takes some twists and turns.

CHAPTER 6

Like Rain on Your Wedding Day

It seems like everywhere I look on Instagram today, someone is talking about creating a "core memory" with their child. I guess it's the new term for an experience that will become permanently etched in their brain—something they'll remember for the rest of their life. If you're a child of the 1970s, an example might be your parents kicking you out of the house during the summer and telling you to drink out of the hose if you got thirsty. In these modern days of kinder, gentler parenting, the discussion of the importance of a core memory might just be a parental device to justify paying for a three-year-old to go to Disney World, but whatever. Everyone has the right to create their own unique brand of misery.

Anyway, a core memory for me is the wedding of Prince Charles to Lady Diana Spencer. Bonus for my parents that this memory was created in our family room on our large console TV for free dollars. I was mesmerized by Diana as she emerged from that real-life Cinderella carriage, wearing a white dress that seemed to go on forever, and walked down the aisle toward her very own Prince Charming. I was ten years old, and it was like watching a real live Disney movie play out before the world.

I mean, we've all watched *The Crown* and know the cold, hard truth about the dynamics between Charles and Diana. (Also, we can probably all agree that the casting directors for season 5 of *The Crown* did Prince Charles a huge favor.) It's funny to me that, even all these years later, I can know the truth and still wish there had been a happier ending to what seemed like a fairy tale back when we were all young and innocent and knew nothing of Camilla Parker Bowles and tawdry phone conversations.

All that to say, somewhere deep inside me, I began dreaming of my own wedding day from the moment I saw Diana in that diamond tiara and train that stretched the length of St. Paul's Cathedral. At the time, that mainly involved thinking about what my own wedding dress would look like rather than who I would marry, because I wasn't even old enough to date yet. Also, my first order of business for any life event has always been to figure out what I'm going to wear.

I will spare you the details of my dating history and the messiness that was contained therein and just fast-forward to the spring of 1997. Perry Shankle proposed to me on April 24 and then immediately asked how soon we could get married and if it could be before hunting season, because priorities. Our wedding date was set for August 16, 1997.

Yes, I planned a wedding in under four months, and to this day it ranks as one of my greatest accomplishments. My mother-in-law told me there was no way to plan a wedding that fast, and I told her, in the words of Jerry Reed from his classic song "East Bound and Down,"[1] "We gonna do what they say can't be done."

God had led me to a great guy, and I couldn't wait to be his wife. The problem was that every time I thought about my wedding, I had flashbacks to my pledge presentation in college when, for five minutes, I'd thought I wanted to be in a sorority. It had felt like a huge deal. Mom and Nanny made the trip to College Station and took me immediately to the mall to find a dress. We had the best time as I tried on a variety of dresses that were all made of velvet with puffy sleeves because this was the early nineties. Everything was great right up until we ran into my dad and stepmom as we were walking out of Dillard's. My mom's mood immediately changed. She no longer wanted to go to dinner; she needed to go back to the hotel because she had a migraine. The whole weekend shifted to being about her and trying to keep her happy, but none of my efforts worked. She ended up missing the entire pledge presentation the next evening because, as she explained after she showed up for the last ten minutes of the night, she "just couldn't do it."

I knew that wedding festivities meant my mom and dad would find themselves in the same room for various celebrations, and that was always something to be dreaded. Suzanne would certainly have a headache or meltdown or be furious with me over her perception that I was ignoring her in favor of my dad. I'd never wished more that there was some sort of map to navigate all the land mines, because experience had taught me explosions were most assuredly on the horizon. So it was with that knowledge at the forefront of my mind that I began to plan my wedding with hopes of keeping the drama to a minimum.

Early in the wedding planning, my mom negotiated that her financial contribution would be to buy my dress, so I made the trip to Beaumont to shop for one with her and Nanny. I'd already shopped for a wedding dress once before in 1993 during my unfortunate brief engagement to a different guy—an engagement that proved to be both a cautionary tale of what not to do and the reason I had store credit at Kay's Bridal Boutique in Beaumont.

During that engagement, wedding dresses had leaned toward a style that can best be described as "Alexis Carrington Gets Married." (This is a reference to the nighttime eighties soap opera *Dynasty*. It lives rent-free in my head.) The sleeves were enormous and puffy. Sparkles were sewn into every piece of fabric possible. The original dress was something like a cross between Princess Diana and Hope Brady when she married Bo on *Days of Our Lives*. But now my eyes had seen the glory of the wedding of Carolyn Bessette to John F. Kennedy, Jr., and I knew something about beautiful simplicity.

I walked out of the dressing room in a simple cream-colored satin dress with a pin-tucked, fitted bodice and full, unadorned skirt. That was the dress. I twirled in front of the full-length mirror while the bridal shop employees all gave it a little applause. I'd never felt better about myself than I did in that dress. I'd tried on a few others that all felt too fussy or precious, but that one felt like me.

Suzanne met my eye in the mirror and said, "I don't really like it. It's too simple." Yes, that was exactly what I was going for.

Treading carefully, I responded, "Really? That's why I like it. It feels timeless."

The saleslady, either sensing my desperation or trying to make a sale, chimed in, "I could tell the minute she walked out that this was the dress. She lit up in this one!" And then, God bless her, she went and found a veil to go with it and began to put the whole look together as she hustled to win my mom over to our side.

I was completely sold. "This is the one! It's exactly what I want."

My mom sat there in silence until she realized we were all waiting on her to say something. "Well, it's more money than I was wanting to spend. Especially on such a plain dress."

The saleslady continued her sales pitch. "I know it seems simple, but this is the look all the brides are wanting right now. It's the Carolyn Bessette effect."

Is it possible this saleslady was my soulmate?

I can only assume the pressure got to my mom, because she finally agreed that this could be the dress, and I thanked her profusely for it all the way back to Nanny's house. Later, I showed her pictures of all the dresses I'd loved in *Brides* magazine so she could see how similar they were to what I'd chosen.

I loved my choice and was sure to let my mom know how much I appreciated her buying it for me, especially because she kept reminding me it was more than she'd wanted to spend. At one point, I even offered to pay her back for the difference between what it cost and what she'd hoped to pay. I instinctively knew I needed to do some damage control because it felt like something that was going to come back around at some point. It's said that history is our best teacher, and history had taught me that there were going to be some consequences for choosing a dress Suzanne didn't like. She had this way of letting something sit for a while so you thought it was all going to be okay, but the more she thought about it, the madder she would get as she built the situation up in her mind.

Which is why I was only a little surprised when my cell-phone rang a week later and it was my mom. I was sitting in the Target parking lot, about to run in to grab some toothpaste and probably $150 of other stuff I didn't know I needed until I saw it in the store. I sensed something was coming as soon as I heard the tone of her voice after I said hello.

"Melanie, I've been thinking about something," she began. This statement alone was enough to send a searing jolt of panic into my chest, because there was usually not much worse than my mom's response to something after she'd had several days to stew about it. "You really didn't seem to appreciate me buying that dress for you and how much it cost. It feels like you don't really want me to be part of this wedding at all, so I'm thinking I probably won't come."

You know how there are moments you think you're prepared for and then they come and you're like, *Nope, did not see that one coming?* This was one of those moments for me.

I inhaled deeply, then said, "Of course I want you at my wedding! And I love the dress. It's just perfect. Thank you so much for buying it for me! Do you want me to pay for part of it?" Because this was a bomb I wasn't sure how to defuse.

"No, you don't have to do that," she responded. "It just seemed like I ended up buying a dress I didn't really like."

Fair point. But also, I was the bride.

Let's discuss how great it feels for your mother to repeatedly tell you how much she dislikes the dress you chose. Nothing makes a bride feel more special than someone saying, "Well, it's not my favorite," as opposed to "You're stunning" or "Wow, you are the most beautiful bride I've ever seen." Those are things that a normal mother would say in that moment when she sees her daughter in a wedding gown. I was also in charge of planning my entire wedding, from the flowers to the food to the venue, because she showed no interest in being involved in any of those details.

And this is where I have to take a minute to share a realization I had a long time ago as I wrestled with Suzanne's repeated accusations that I never wanted her around or never let her get involved in any part of my life. In hindsight, I see clearly that I was like that because she was never safe for me. I desperately wanted a mom who would support me and cheer me on and encourage me in the ways only a mom can, but I learned that wasn't *my* mom. Everything with her seemed to backfire painfully, so I began to look for that safe place in other people God brought into my life.

A few months later, my wedding day arrived. I'd planned a noon wedding in August, which should be an indicator of how in love I was with Perry. I woke up early to get married during the hottest part of the summer. There is no love as willing to sacrifice who you really are as young love. These days, I would never agree to a noon wedding, largely because age has brought me two deep vertical wrinkles that appear across my forehead each morning and make me look like I've been attacked by Lord Voldemort while I slept.

The day started with a trip to the hair salon, where my hair was put in an elaborate updo and also where I impulsively decided to get bangs cut on my wedding day. Why am I the way that I am? Who thinks that's a good idea hours before one of the biggest moments of one's life? Me, apparently. My new bangs and I headed to the church to finish getting ready in the bridal room with my bridesmaids. I could feel the love and joy in that room as my closest friends and I did our makeup and touched up our hair and traded compliments about how beautiful we all looked. It was reminiscent of all the times we did that in college as we prepared to go out for the night. But now we were all grown up, and I was about to walk down the aisle toward the man I'd hoped and prayed to find. It was one of the happiest days I could remember. Then it was time for me to put on my dress, but my mom wasn't there yet.

That presented a dilemma.

I could wait for Suzanne to arrive before I put on my dress, which meant the entire wedding would run behind schedule. Or I could go ahead and have my friends and stepmom help me into my dress, which meant there would be hell to pay when and if Suzanne showed up.

I chose option A, which meant that I began to obsessively check the time every five minutes to see how close we were getting to the point when I would need to accept that my mom wasn't coming. Finally, forty-five minutes after she was supposed to arrive and after multiple people tried to call her and find out where she was, my mother sauntered into the room, waving to everyone as though she were queen of the Rose Parade.

"Sorry I'm late!" she chirped. "But I woke up with the worst headache and had to find a chiropractor to come to the hotel and work on me." It was reminiscent of what she'd done so many times before, and my special day became more about praying she wasn't about to spoil it. And I knew that somehow it all went back to my wedding dress.

But what do you do on your wedding day when your mom shows up late? You dry your tears, check to make sure your mascara isn't smeared, and decide to be thankful she showed up at all.

The rest of the day was everything I'd hoped it would be. I became Mrs. Perry Shankle. A new chapter of my life was beginning, and I was full of gratitude for what I foolishly believed was my finally escaping the hold my mom had on me. After all, I was a full-fledged married woman now. A bona fide grown-up.

If only it had been that easy.

After the professional photographs came back from the wedding, Suzanne and I were perusing them and deciding what to order. She looked at one of her and me and pointedly said, "See how your head is tilting away from me in that picture? You didn't want me to be there."

And something in me died as I realized I was never going to win that battle. I also didn't have the emotional capacity to say what I wanted to scream at the top of my lungs, "You held that day hostage, and I am just trying to keep it together in that photo because I didn't want to ruin the day."

But I didn't say that, because it was a battle I wasn't yet ready to fight.

CHAPTER 7

Sparkle and Spackle

Perry and I celebrated our twenty-fifth wedding anniversary last year, otherwise known as our silver anniversary. I'm going to assume it's called silver because being married for twenty-five years means we both have gray hair, even though one of us chooses to color our hair to keep it brown. I'll let you decide who, although here's a hint: A man with gray hair might be referred to as a "silver fox," whereas a woman with gray hair might be referred to as an "old hag." Don't blame me; blame our youth-obsessed society.

The morning of our anniversary, I found myself looking through our wedding album because I was feeling nostalgic. I showed a couple of pictures to Perry and said, "Look at us! We had no idea all the life that was ahead. Do you even remember being those two young people?"

For a few seconds, he looked at a picture of us cutting our wedding cake, and I waited to hear his deepest thoughts on this life we've built together and the lessons we've learned over twenty-five years. He finally said, "All I know is if you put that chocolate cake in front of me right now, I'd eat the whole thing."

Thank you for coming to Perry's breakout session on twenty-five years of marriage.

The reality is, marriage is a leap of faith. In our case, God put a planner and a dreamer together—someone who is always prepared for every scenario and someone who believes things will magically work out. He's up before the sun rises, and my day doesn't really start until noon. He's an extrovert who's never met a stranger, and I sometimes hide from people I know in the grocery store. He brings the spackle; I bring the sparkle. He makes life practical; I make it pretty. And against all odds and by the grace of God, it has worked for us.

He's everything I waited my whole life to find—not because it's always been easy, but because I have someone who is always on my side, even when he doesn't agree with me. As a girl who spent the first part of her life dreaming of a normal-ish family and a house filled with love, I've seen God fulfill that dream.

Please don't take all this to mean we have a perfect marriage. There is no such thing. There was a time in the early days when I got so mad at him during a fight that I threw our cordless phone against a wall and watched it shatter. But you learn and grow. I would never do anything like that now, because we've mellowed with age. (And also, throwing something that hard might cause the arthritis in my shoulder to flare up.)

But let's go back to the beginning of our marriage.

We spent our first year settling into married life, and even though it had its ups and downs (please see the paragraph above about me throwing a phone), we were off to a great start. We bought our first house together, and my goal from the beginning was to make it a home that we could grow old in, and—spoiler alert—we still live in this same house. Everything in me wanted to put down roots and build something that would stand the test of time, so we worked hard to make that happen. By that time, Perry was well aware of all the dysfunction I'd come from, and we set out to intentionally break those cycles. All those unhealthy patterns were going to end with us.

I'd read all the statistics and studies that showed that children of divorce were more likely to end up divorced themselves, and I guess those numbers are true. But I felt as though everything I'd been through as a kid made me that much more determined that I would make our marriage work—and not just work but thrive. I also knew there was going to be a learning curve for me because I hadn't grown up watching healthy day-to-day relationships play out. Over those first couple of years, we just settled into what can best be described as normal married life, and I was as content and happy as I could ever remember being up to that point.

About a year into our marriage, I decided to fly to Oklahoma to see my mom for the weekend. I hadn't seen her much since the wedding, and I felt like it might be time for a visit, mainly because she kept calling and making me feel bad about it. She picked me up from the airport, and we had fun catching up over dinner before arriving at the new house she and her husband had bought a few years earlier. From the time I walked in the door, I could feel the tension. James made it clear by his icy reception that he didn't want me to be there and walked back to their bedroom shortly after my arrival.

I decided to do my best to just ignore his behavior and try to enjoy the time with my mom. I went into the kitchen to pop some popcorn so we could settle in and watch a movie together. But that's when my mom informed me that James didn't allow anyone to eat in the living room and we'd need to eat our popcorn in the kitchen before the movie started.

Why is he raining on my popcorn parade? What is going on?

We sat and watched our movie sans popcorn, like they probably do in hell, and then went to bed. The next morning at breakfast, my mom waited until James walked out of the kitchen. Then she whispered, "You left the hall light on last night, and he doesn't like that. He asked if you were having some kind of party. Will you please make sure you turn it off tonight?"

Oh yes. The infamous hall-light parties you always hear people talk about.

I knew I was at my mom's house because the furniture I grew up with was there. But that house was most definitely not any kind of home to me. I began counting down the hours until it would be time to head to the airport. I called Perry that night to check in, and he delivered the worst news imaginable: "Hey, it's been raining here ever since you left on Friday, and everything is flooded. Your flight is probably going to get canceled."

Let me tell you that I have never thought more about the possibility of catching a bus to Texas and then finding a rowboat to rent. I just wanted to get home to my husband, to a living room where I was allowed to eat on the couch and a place where I didn't feel like I might end up on *Dateline.*

After I went to bed that night, I could hear my mom and James fighting in the other room. Something crashed and then a door slammed. I lay there and wondered if I was about to be murdered in my sleep. I closed my eyes and prayed that God would protect my mom and me. I also vowed that if I made it home to San Antonio alive the next day, I would never return to that house.

And I will tell you that both of those things happened. My flight was miraculously on time, and I never went back to Oklahoma.

· · · · · ·

The other night, Perry asked me what I would go back and change about our marriage if I could. Initially, I thought my answer would be something like "I would change that you will never one time be able to find the ketchup in the fridge without my assistance." But then I decided to dive a little deeper and said, "I wish I would've learned earlier on to be myself and express what mattered to me and how I actually felt about things." I didn't really know how to do that. I'd grown up hiding my feelings because there wasn't room for them while I lived with Suzanne. My goal at all times was to try to keep everything as calm as possible. I lived in a constant state of "Don't anger it." The times when I would express to her that I was unhappy about a situation, I was usually met with a sarcastic "Poor little Melanie. Nothing ever goes her way." So I learned to just keep my mouth shut.

I hadn't meant to bring those things into my marriage, but the people pleaser in me had been forged by my first eighteen years. It turns out that wasn't just something that living on my own or being married could fix. It took me many years to figure out that it was okay to voice discontent or disagree with someone I loved. It didn't mean they were going to leave me or discount how I felt. The truth was, most arguments Perry and I had in the early days of our marriage involved him telling me, "I am not a mind reader." Which is unfortunate but fair.

This is still something I struggle with at times, and maybe this feels familiar to you too. *Heaven forbid I inconvenience anyone, so instead, I will just lie here and bleed out on the side of the road.* The problem arises when I bottle up my feelings for way too long, which then tends to lead to an outburst of epic proportions that could have been avoided if I'd just had a hard conversation. I've spent years learning that people who love you do want to know how you feel or if they've hurt you in some way. What a concept.

When we got married, Perry didn't exactly realize how toxic the dynamic was between my mom and me, but he quickly learned, because there are things you can't hide when you and your spouse live in the same house. He saw the stress on my face when I picked up the phone and it was Suzanne on the other end of the line. He knew I dreaded her visits since I never knew what mean comment was going to come flying out of her mouth. It wasn't even that these things were always terrible, but there was the possibility of her going off the rails that kept me on edge whenever she was involved.

We had been married about three years when she came to stay with us several times in the months leading up to my sister's San Antonio wedding. I helped Amy plan most of the details because we both knew Suzanne wouldn't be capable of taking care of all that goes into a wedding, but that also caused resentment. One afternoon, we were getting ready to leave for a wedding shower for Amy. Gulley and her husband, Jon, were at the house, along with Perry and my mom. They were all waiting for me to finish getting ready, and when I walked into the kitchen wearing a new outfit I'd bought for the occasion, my mom looked at me and said, "You look like a streetwalker." My face flushed with embarrassment, and I looked down as if taking inventory of my outfit: a pair of black pants embroidered with hot pink flowers, and a matching sweater top. In my general opinion, clothing that came from Harold's typically wasn't considered streetwalker apparel. Equestrian aficionado, maybe, but not really streetwalker vibes. What she'd said was a tangible expression of the way she resented the happiness and peace I'd found in my new life.

That resentment was confirmed a few days later when I was having lunch with Amy to talk about wedding details. We were discussing the past weekend and our assessment of how Suzanne had behaved overall. I told her about the streetwalker comment, and Amy said, "Yeah, she told me later that night that you had been telling her how happy you were and how good life seemed for you right now, and she said she was tired of you bragging about things." That was such a moment of clarity for me. It had never occurred to me that she wouldn't want to hear about my life and how things were going. Because what mother doesn't want to hear that her child is happy and doing well? As a mom myself, I know the old saying is true that a mother is only as happy as her most miserable child. And I count as a huge win every moment that my daughter is content and happy.

Maybe that weekend and Amy getting married became the catalyst for Suzanne to really outdo herself, because, a couple of months later, I had a voicemail from Nanny asking me to call her when I had some time to talk. I called her back as soon as I heard her message, because something in her voice told me it was important. This was confirmed when she started the call with "I have something to tell you, and I need you to be okay with it." Nanny stumbled over her words for a minute, not really saying anything, until she said, "So, back in 1966, your mom got pregnant and had a baby."

When I say that I had to put my head between my knees to keep from blacking out, I am not lying. My mind began to spin as I wondered if Nanny was about to tell me that I wasn't my dad's biological child even though I look just like him. Any bomb seemed possible at that moment, and Nanny's trembling voice didn't reassure me in the least. She continued, "She got pregnant the summer after she graduated from high school. I had no idea until she came home from college later that fall and finally confessed to me that she was pregnant. I didn't know what to do, so I sent her back to college until Christmas break to finish out the semester.

"And then when she came home at Christmas, I just told her she would need to stay hidden in her bedroom so no one would find out. I told everyone, including your Big Bob, that she was sick and couldn't go back to school. I found a doctor I trusted to keep this secret, and when she went into labor late one night, I drove her to his office, where she delivered the baby. She had a baby girl, and the nurse who helped with delivery ended up adopting her."

Well, this brand-new information was certainly a lot to process on a Tuesday afternoon. Let me count the things I had to wrap my brain around in about forty-five seconds:

My mom had a secret baby that no one knew about.
Nanny hid my mom in the back bedroom and told literally

no one about this, which feels like a thing that could cause some trauma.

I had an older sister whom I'd never met.

The shame beyond belief my mom heaped on me and the way she told me I'd ruined myself when she discovered I'd slept with my high school boyfriend seemed very hypocritical at this moment.

But wait. There's more.

"Your mom doesn't know I'm calling to tell you all this, so please don't tell her I told you. But she decided a few months ago that she wanted to look for her daughter, and she's found her. We went to go meet her in person last week, and now your mom is planning to tell you and Amy about it this weekend when she comes to visit. And, Melanie, you need to be okay with this, and you need to set an example to make Amy okay with it."

Sure, no pressure.

This was how it always was with my mom. Just when you thought you'd gotten to the bottom of all the secrets, lo, there were even more deep, dark ones to be exposed.

Nanny explained where my new half sister had been all those years, where she'd grown up, and where she currently lived. She was in her early thirties, married with two boys of her own. As it turns out, she'd grown up fewer than fifty miles from where we lived in Beaumont and had known who my mom was the whole time but had chosen to never make contact. She'd been adopted by a lovely couple who went on to have four biological kids, and she appeared to have a good life. I was too wrapped up in my own feelings about all that to wonder how this young woman felt about my mom deciding to enter her life, although that thought would occur to me later.

I hung up the phone and walked into the living room, where Perry was waiting to talk to me. He'd heard enough of the conversation to know it was something major. I began crying and put my head in my hands as I collapsed into a chair and announced between sobs, "My mom had a baby in 1966, put her up for adoption, and now she's found her. I have a sister I knew nothing about, and now my mom wants me to meet her."

Perry looked at me for a second and then said, "Does this mean we have to buy your new sister a Christmas present?"

Ladies and gentlemen, this is why I married Perry Shankle.

Sometimes funny trumps everything.

· · · · · ·

The weekend after the phone call that was basically "Surprise! You have a big sister," I went to Dallas to see Amy. My mom was going to drive in from Oklahoma later in the weekend, so I had an evening with Amy to figure out a way to break the news that we had a new sister. After dinner with Amy and her husband, Chris, we went back to their apartment and were sitting in the living room when I cleared my throat and said, "So, Nanny called me last week, and I have something to tell you about Mom."

Amy looked at me expectantly, because experience had taught both of us this was probably not going to be some small thing. "Well," I began, "it turns out Mom had a baby back in 1966, put her up for adoption, and has now found her. That's why she's coming here this weekend . . . to tell us all about it."

To his credit, Chris got up from his chair at this point and just left the room. Truthfully, I wanted to go with him. I proceeded to tell Amy all that I knew about our new sister as I heeded Nanny's pleas to encourage her to have a positive outlook regarding this new development. *A long-lost sister! What a delight this will be! Mom will no doubt handle this beautifully!*

But then I heard myself say something to Amy that I absolutely believed to be true at that time: "Here's the thing: I know this is a lot to take in, but what if this has been the source of all her unhappiness over the years? I can't even imagine the trauma of keeping something like this a secret. What if finding the daughter she gave up is the very thing that will finally bring her some peace and help her be happy? I think we need to do our best to let her know that we totally understand and support all of this."

Amy agreed with me, so when Mom got into town and delivered what she certainly felt was going to be a huge emotional blow to both of us, we told her how much we loved her, that we couldn't imagine how hard that had been to keep secret all those years, and that of course we would love to meet her other daughter.

I didn't realize until much later how many times I told myself that over the years. It was my mantra: *Maybe this will be the thing that makes her better. Maybe this marriage, maybe this relationship, maybe this good behavior on my part, maybe if I just act like everything is okay, maybe if I just give up what I really want to do and do what she wants . . .* It was all about trying to find the key to her unhappiness and unlocking the door to her peace and stability. And it always proved to be an impossible task.

Have you ever been in a relationship with someone where you kept waiting and hoping that something was going to bring about a big change? The one with my mom was my version of being Charlie Brown while Lucy moves the football over and over again. There are some balls you won't ever be able to kick, and, well, that's a real kick in the pants.

Any peace that Suzanne felt from being reunited with her daughter was as short-lived as each of the events that came before that. Amy and I met our half sister that Christmas, and she was and is a lovely person. In reality, she had a great life long before my mom reentered the picture, and she wasn't looking to be rescued from anything. I believe Suzanne found that to be a great disappointment. She was wanting to swoop into this girl's life thirtysomething years later and be some sort of hero, and that wasn't going to be the case. So she began to do to her what she'd always done to us: She picked apart her flaws, highlighted the ways she felt she wasn't what she expected or needed her to be, and then just moved on to the next thing as though my half sister were a toy that no longer brought any value.

A few months later, I was at Nanny's house, visiting for the weekend, and Mom was there. I needed to borrow her laptop to send an email, and when I opened it up, I found a message she'd drafted to her eldest daughter. I'm not sure if she ever actually sent it or not, but what she'd written included this sentence: "I wanted to find you because I hoped we could have a relationship. My own daughters have been a disappointment to me in so many ways, and I thought things could be different with you."

And there you have it.

That was the point when I finally realized that the thing I'd been hoping would heal her or fix her was never going to come. She was broken beyond what anyone could repair, and I was done trying. And that realization set me free in ways I didn't even recognize at the time.

CHAPTER 8

Sweet Caroline

One thing I always knew was that I wanted to be a mom. Not because I necessarily loved children, since, by and large, I'm not really a person who's great with babies or little kids. I mean, they're fine and all, but you can't really have a great discussion about thermonuclear physics and shows on Netflix with them. (I'll let you guess which one I like to talk about more.)

Perry and I had been married about five years when we decided we were ready to bring a baby into this equation. Gulley and Jon had just had their first baby, and this only amplified my feelings that I wanted one of my own. So Perry and I had the conversation where we decided we were officially on the trying-to-conceive train, a conversation he later confessed made him feel like he was going to either throw up or hurl himself out of a moving vehicle, as he measured the weight of what we were about to take on.

Initially, I had a breezier view of parenthood. How hard could it be? You don't even have to get a license to do it.

Let me tell you how this attitude went for me.

I got pregnant exactly the first month we quit using any form of contraception, which only confirmed my belief that this parenting thing was going to be so much easier than people led me to believe. And then six weeks after we saw that positive test, Perry and I were in the doctor's office holding each other's hand as the doctor explained that the ultrasound revealed our baby had ceased to have a heartbeat at the ten-week mark. We were devastated. All of a sudden, a fraction of the full weight of what it means to be a mother settled into my heart. The pure, raw love you have for something that ultimately you have no control over really defies understanding or any real description of how it feels until you experience it. Losing this baby we already loved so much gave me a glimpse of that.

The morning I had my D&C, Gulley showed up at the hospital and sat with Perry while he waited for the procedure to be over. All I remember of that day is a deep, aching sadness and asking Perry to drive me through Shipley's on our way home from the hospital so I could get a chocolate-covered doughnut, as one does in any time of grief. I'd called my mom to let her know about the miscarriage and the D&C, and she showed up about two weeks after the fact. Truthfully, I didn't even want her to come, as I was deep in the throes of sadness, but she insisted that she wanted to see me.

That weekend as we were running errands in my car, I tried to share with her what happened, how I felt, and some additional health issues the miscarriage had revealed. I glanced over to where she sat in the passenger seat, because I could tell she wasn't paying any attention to what I was saying, and saw her frantically digging through her purse. "What are you looking for?" I asked with a sigh of deep exasperation and frustration.

"I just really need a piece of gum," she replied.

Okay.

Okay, then.

Right then and there I made a mental note: *Do not under any circumstances ever decide that a piece of gum is the most pressing issue when my future child is telling me something important.*

That miscarriage turned out to be a molar pregnancy, which required medical intervention to get my body back to normal. When I finally got pregnant seven months later, we were excited but apprehensive. I'd gotten a little experience with how precarious life could be, so I monitored my pregnancy with an intensity usually reserved for lab experiments.

Do I know anything about lab experiments? I do not. Science isn't my thing. But it felt like an accurate metaphor, so please allow it.

When I finally got to the six-month mark of pregnancy, we knew we were having a girl, and it was time to celebrate. Our friends planned multiple showers, and I strategically invited my mom to the one I felt would be safest to have her at. It was being held at a girlfriend's house, and I decided to invite only my mom and not my stepmom to eliminate any potential drama. The day of the shower arrived, and everything was beautiful. I felt so loved and so thankful for this new baby who was about to enter our lives.

Then Amy showed up to the shower with my mom, who was clearly drugged out of her mind. She was slurring her words, making inappropriate comments, and just generally being a combination of volatile and out of it. Thankfully, my mother-in-law and Gulley recognized what was happening and spent the next couple of hours managing that whole situation, but

Suzanne had succeeded yet again in making the day all about her.

My mom spent that night at my house. Gulley came over to hang out and, frankly, be a buffer for me. We'd also come up with a plan for Gulley to sneak into the guest bedroom where my mom was staying to try to take inventory of all the meds she had in her possession. I'd had an idea that she was taking a lot of prescription drugs, but the baby shower confirmed it was worse than I'd thought. Gulley completed her assignment like she was Sydney Bristow on a mission to take down SD-6 and even wrote everything down so we could reference it later to figure out what some of the generic pill names meant. And I tell you no lies when I say the list was an extensive array of benzodiazepines, opioids, and antidepressants. That doesn't even include pills that were in nameless prescription bottles and couldn't be identified. They were from different pharmacies and prescribed by various doctors, and the dates seemed to indicate it was a collection of pharmaceuticals she'd amassed over the years.

As for Gulley's reconnaissance work, are you even a real friend if you haven't sifted through your friend's mom's bag of pills? Where does that fall in the love languages?

My mom and I met Amy for lunch the next day. I'd informed my sister about all the pills during a late-night phone conversation, and we decided we'd talk to her about it while we were all together. But the minute we broached the subject, it became apparent it was a nonstarter. "Oh, I'm fine," Mom said, clearly annoyed at us for getting in her business. "Those are just the pills I need to manage my neck pain. My doctor knows all about them."

Her abrupt answer created an awkwardness as we all finished our lunch, unsure what else to say. But then Mom pulled out her checkbook, wrote a check, and handed it to me as she said, "You can use this money to buy a crib for the baby. This is my gift." I took the check and thanked her for it as I told her I already knew the exact crib I wanted to buy. We all sat there for a few more minutes before she pulled out her checkbook again and wrote Amy a check for the same amount. She handed it to her and said, "This is for you because at least you'll appreciate it."

I never had the right reaction for my mom. To this day, I still sometimes worry about my reactions because I'm so afraid that people won't think I really appreciate them or am grateful for some kindness they have shown. But then I have to make sure I don't seem overly zealous lest it look insincere, which is as exhausting as it sounds. In truth, I wish we could all react like Kristen Wiig as the overenthusiastic Sue from *Saturday Night Live* and just respond to everything with "I'm so freakin' excited!" as we crash through a window.

Later that evening, after my mom had flown back to Oklahoma, I sat down with Perry and we recapped the weekend together. We already had concerns about my mom being around the new baby once she arrived, and the weekend had absolutely confirmed that for us. Not to mention, I knew I didn't want her at the hospital when I went into labor, because it would just add more stress, but then that decision stressed me out because I knew I would never hear the end of it after the fact.

But when I went into labor a few months later and experienced what labor pains truly were, I knew for sure I couldn't handle my mom being there. It already felt like a fight was going on inside my uterus, and I didn't have the strength or desire for any other pain at that critical moment. There wasn't enough air in the hospital room for all my emotions combined with whatever my mom would bring to the table, so we let all our people know that the baby was arriving but made the decision to call my mom after the fact. The good news was she would have to get a flight and figure out travel logistics, so we knew that would buy us at least a day or so after the baby arrived.

Caroline Tatum Shankle showed up two weeks early, weighing in at a whopping five pounds. She was the tiniest little thing I'd ever seen, and I was overwhelmed with love. This was my daughter. I had a daughter. At that moment, it felt like all I ever wanted in life. That first morning, when the pediatric nurse brought her to my hospital room, she told me that Caroline was having a hard time getting warm because she was so tiny. She suggested we do skin-to-skin contact because that would help her regulate her body temperature. I unwrapped her from her pink blanket and marveled at her little hands and feet as I laid her on my chest. We began to breathe in and out together as she snuggled up against me and slept. It was one of the most holy moments of my life. The fact that God had entrusted me with this little girl felt unfathomable, but I knew with everything in my heart that I was going to do everything I could to not let Him or Caroline down. I would protect her to the best of my ability. I would raise her to be strong and resilient and to live in the security that comes with knowing you are fiercely loved and adored. I was going to be the mother to her that I'd desperately wanted for myself.

When my mom showed up at the hospital the next day, I

reluctantly handed Caroline over to her. She held her for a few minutes, and then I cringed as she began to unswaddle her. She declared, "Well, her fingernails are too long and need to be cut. Where are the nail clippers?" I looked at Perry because I felt helpless lying there twelve hours post-birth in nothing but my mesh underwear and a pajama top. But allowing my mom to have any kind of sharp object anywhere near my baby was about to make me stand straight up out of that hospital bed. Perry walked over, took Caroline from my mom, and handed her back to me as he said, "I think her fingernails are fine for now."

That moment was another layer in the unraveling of our relationship. The thought crystallizing in my mind was that it was no longer about me just protecting myself; it was about protecting my own daughter. That changed the game forever.

CHAPTER 9

The Joy of My Life

I was just about to start writing this chapter when I got a text from Caroline. She was in need of a pair of shoes that would go with black pants for her new job and wanted my opinion. This is my wheelhouse. I live to give out any sort of fashion advice to anyone and everyone. I gave her my thoughts, including maybe a chunky-soled loafer. She sent me back a GIF of a dancing pilgrim and said those shoes would make her look like she both dresses to impress and is also fighting for religious freedom under the British regime. The Bible says, "I have no greater joy than to hear that my children are walking in the truth" (3 John 4, ESV). Let me also submit Melanie 1:1: "I have no greater joy than to know that my child is hilarious and quick-witted." Being Caroline's mom is truly the joy of my life.

One of the things Perry and I talked about a lot during my pregnancy with her was being purposeful with our parenting and committing every step of the way to seeking God and following His voice concerning our daughter. Both of us had come from families that didn't allow us to always be our real selves, and we wanted to raise Caroline in the freedom to be exactly who God made her to be. I knew from my own childhood that so much of what you grow up believing about yourself is what your parents tell you. From the beginning, we wanted Caroline to know that her whole, true self was all we wanted or expected her to be. And we knew that couldn't happen unless we intentionally broke generational cycles that weren't going to serve the way we hoped to raise her.

In the early days with Caroline, life was all pretty simple—I mean, other than the fact that I was sometimes so sleep deprived that I couldn't remember if I'd showered or not. The first three months of having a newborn is really like carrying around an eight-pound bag of sugar that occasionally poops all over you and keeps you up all night. But the one thing I did consistently was pray over her life during all those late-night feedings when it was just the two of us in her pink nursery. I knew the kind of mom I wanted to be, but I also knew I wasn't going to be able to do it without placing God at the forefront of every decision. In those wee hours of the morning as we rocked back and forth, I prayed for everything that came to mind for her life. I prayed that she would be strong and brave. I prayed that she would always seek God first. I prayed for her future friends and her future husband. I prayed for wisdom to lead her in the ways that she should go. I prayed that we would always be close and that she would never have a moment of not knowing she was loved beyond measure. I wanted her life to be drenched in the goodness of God so that she would never doubt His love for her.

As Caroline grew and began to turn into a real little person, Perry and I started to see some of our prayers for her become reality. She was most definitely strong-willed. She had a mind of her own and wasn't afraid to speak up for herself or for someone else. I enrolled her in preschool two days a week when she turned two, and when I went to pick her up that first day, her teacher told me, "She refused to take a nap, so I might need you to pick her up before nap time every day so she doesn't spend that time trying to keep the other kids awake." Yes, I saw that coming. She was always a kid who believed sleep is for the weak. But that was the beginning of my helping Caroline navigate the world around her. When I explained to her she couldn't stay for nap time unless she would lie there quietly and let the other kids sleep, she agreed to do it and she did. It was clear early on that she wasn't going to comply unless she was given a practical reason behind the rules. But she was also charming and funny enough to get away with it. By Christmas break, the same preschool teacher who once threatened to kick her out over nap-time noncompliance wrote me a note that read, "Caroline is a delight to have in class! She makes us all laugh every day and is just the best conversationalist!"

She was two.

What was Caroline talking about? The current price of oil?

Every morning, I would dress her in a cute outfit and put big bows in her hair, and by the time I picked her up every afternoon, she looked like a sorority girl who had stayed too long at the keg party. Her bows were nowhere to be found, her hair was flying everywhere in a tangled mess, and her outfit was covered in various stains that told the story of what she'd eaten and what color paint she'd used for craft time. If there had only been a preschool version of *Bama Rush* TikTok doing OOTD (that stands for "outfit of the day," for those of us born before the year

2000), because Caroline's would have been "My dress is Gap-Kids, my shoes are Gymboree, my mustache is Kool-Aid, and all the sand in my diaper is from where I dug a giant hole on the playground and put the stuff down my pants."

She was never a delicate flower. Her preschool teachers told me at the end of the school year that the first thing Caroline did each morning as she walked into the classroom was take the bows out of her hair and hand them to the teachers for safe-keeping while saying, "No, thank you."

When I found out we were having a girl, I was definitely overwhelmed with doubts about whether I'd be a good mom. However, I also initially thought somehow that I'd be raising a mini version of myself. I envisioned lots of pink, baby dolls, and Barbies. There would be dance recitals and perhaps a cheerleader in my future. And, friend, that is not what I got.

She named her first baby doll Cuckoo. She never really cared about Barbie. Her favorite toy was a Crocodile Hunter Steve Irwin action figure that came with a battery-operated remote-control truck and a plastic crocodile. When I signed her up for ballet and foolishly prepaid for the recital that was held in the spring, I had to bribe her every week to go to class. After the recital, where she just stood onstage the whole time and barely moved, she announced, "I won that whole thing. I beat all those other girls." Her favorite place was outside with her dad doing anything that involved getting covered in mud. Her fashion sense as a child was best described as hobo chic. Her best friends were Gulley's two boys, who were more like her brothers, and that didn't help matters. They wrestled. They fought. They loved nothing more than a prank involving a whoopee cushion. What I'm saying is, she was very different from what I'd imagined her to be back when she was just a dream and not a reality.

But let me tell you, I loved every bit of it. She was an adventure I didn't know I needed. Her view of the world was so new, and I was amazed at the way she could confidently walk into any room and feel free to let everyone know exactly what she wanted. To this day, I always say that she and Perry share the same personality characteristic, which is best summed up by their opinion that if anyone doesn't like them, then there is clearly something wrong with that person. It is magical to see. The times I've silently clapped my hands in delight as I've watched her go about her business are too many to count.

And here's the thing: When I began to see who she was and understand what made her tick, God gave me the wisdom to let her be every bit of herself. It turns out I didn't need to raise a mini version of myself, because what He had given me to raise was so much better. When she was young, we had this little chair that served as her time-out chair. Whenever she did something wrong, we would send her there to give her time to calm down and think about her actions. It never failed that when I went to get her after a few minutes, there would be a puddle of spit on the floor between her feet. I finally watched from a distance and realized that while she sat in time-out, she would angrily spit on the floor the entire time. And you know what? I respected the sentiment behind it. She was obedient enough to know she had to stay in that chair until I came to get her, but she had enough spirit to make it known she wasn't happy about it. God helped me see that was a trait that would take her far in life, and I didn't want to break that will. It just had to be reined in a little at times.

Raising Caroline made me spend a lot of time wondering how different I might have been if I'd been allowed to use my voice more when I was growing up. I realize we are each born with a distinct personality, but how is that personality shaped by our environment? Have you ever wondered that when you look back at your own childhood? When I look now at how quick I am to stand up for myself or make my feelings known, I wonder if that was always part of my personality but I just learned from an early age to stay quiet in an attempt to keep everyone calm. Was this in me all along but buried beneath tons of other things because I felt like I had to keep my mom's world on its axis? Or is it just that now I'm in my early fifties and I'm hot all the time and don't have the time or inclination to suppress my feelings and opinions like I used to?

. . . . . .

One of the best things that happened in the years after Caroline was born was how close I became to my dad and Cherrie. Our relationship had been good for a long time by that point, but watching them become grandparents brought us to a whole new level. They drove to the hospital in the middle of the night to be there when Caroline was born, and it was love at first sight. There has been so much redemption for my dad to get to love his granddaughter without all the complications that came from my mom during my childhood. He and Cherrie made the drive from Houston to San Antonio about twice a month during Caroline's first two years of life and ultimately made the decision to move to San Antonio on what happened to be her second birthday.

They were her Mimi and Bops, and they all adored one another. I have older friends who tell me there isn't much better than being a grandparent, but I have to say there hasn't been much sweeter than watching Dad and Cherrie become grandparents. And I counted on them in those early years in ways that I couldn't articulate. They gave us a break when we needed it, Cherrie always brought the most darling outfits for Caroline to wear, and they were a caring and supportive presence in Caroline's life that I trusted to love and protect her at all costs.

Meanwhile, my mom visited just a couple of times during Caroline's first few years. Having her visit only served to add stress because I couldn't take my eyes off her whenever she was near the baby. I didn't trust her to hold Caroline. It was like giving a toddler a carton full of eggs to carry around: a disaster waiting to happen.

Any time my mom spent with us set Perry and me both on edge, so I was relieved that she really didn't show much interest in visiting more often. And as Caroline grew older, I became less afraid of how my mom could hurt her physically and more concerned about what she could do to her emotionally. Caroline adored her Mimi and Bops, and I worried that if Suzanne knew the depth of those relationships, she would do her best to poison them for Caroline the way she had for me. I wasn't going to have it. I wanted to protect Caroline from what had caused so much emotional damage in my own life, and I wasn't entirely sure how I was going to navigate it all. My mom seemed like a wrecking ball that, at any given moment, could come swinging through everything we were building. And all I knew for sure was I couldn't stand by and let that happen, but I also had no idea how to prevent it.

That was the first time I let myself wonder what life would be like if I ever got the courage to walk away from my relationship with my mom.

CHAPTER 10

No Good Comes in the Comments

Most people who love to write also love to read. I am no exception. From my earliest memory, I devoured every book I was given, and there was really no greater joy than time spent in a B. Dalton Bookseller store at the mall. I loved every book written by Judy Blume and Beverly Cleary. Those women shaped my view of humor and how to tell a funny story. They were my version of childhood heroes and the original influences that made me want to write books. If I could capture the magic I felt the first time I ever read about Fudge Hatcher or Ramona Quimby, I could sell it for at least twenty-five dollars.

Then, when I was about nine or ten years old, I found a book sitting on the end table in our living room. It was a hardcover book with brightly colored cherries all over the cover and a cartoon housewife in a bathrobe lying in the middle of them all. It was *If Life Is a Bowl of Cherries, What Am I Doing in the Pits?* by Erma Bombeck. I can only assume I judged a book by its cover when I picked it up and decided to read it, but nothing prepared me for what was inside. Looking back, I'm not sure why as an elementary school kid I knew to appreciate how brilliant and funny that author was as she wrote about things like carpooling, making dinner, packing lunches, and being married. I just know that reading her words opened a door to a whole new world for me. I discovered her daily column in the newspaper and read it before I left for school every morning. When I look back at the influences that made me want to write, Erma Bombeck is chief among them. She helped me realize that you can make anything funny if you tell it the right way.

So fast-forward to July 2005. Caroline was just a month shy of her third birthday, and I was living my worst life as a pharmaceutical salesperson. It turns out it's hard to sell products to people if you don't enjoy making small talk or, you know, selling things. During my maternity leave, in a quest to compile some quality information about how to get one's baby to sleep through the night, I'd discovered what the people were calling "mommy blogs." It became part of my daily routine to read these posts by normal, everyday women writing about their lives. I was hooked. Part of the attraction was that reading their words made me feel less alone as I navigated being a new mom, but it was also that there was this new avenue for an ordinary person to put their writing out on a public platform that didn't require having a publishing deal. I had wanted to be a writer since childhood but had no idea how to make that a reality. No one, including other writers, really encourages young people to grow up and be writers, because it's basically a job where you pour your heart out over a keyboard and are rewarded with tens of dollars for your trouble, unless you happen to be Danielle Steel or John Grisham.

Reading these mommy blogs is what inspired me late one

night to open a free account on Blogspot.com and create my own blog. On a whim, I called it *Big Mama* because this was back in ye olden days of the internet when if you put your real name out there, you were essentially inviting a band of criminals to come rob your home. I chose *Big Mama* because that was what Caroline had taken to calling me in the months before, due to the fact that I was always telling her what a big girl she was as I worked to get her to give up her pacifier and use the potty. In her mind, *big* was about as great a compliment as you could give someone, and frankly, I felt honored by the name.

As I began to write nightly on my blog, I felt something come alive in me. The blog became a creative outlet for me to write down funny stories about Caroline and our lives. I watched my readership grow as people shared my words with their friends. But the biggest piece for me was getting the chance to find my voice as a writer and create something that felt meaningful. That blog is what led to you (hopefully) paying some American dollars for the book you are holding in your hands. But in the beginning, I was just a girl sitting in front of a computer, asking you to love me.

I'd been writing daily on the blog for about four months when I decided to compose a birthday post as a tribute to my dad on his sixty-first birthday. Here's what I said, since I'm assuming you didn't read it unless you were one of the approximately forty-five daily readers I had back then:

The other day, I was reading an article about the new show called *Heroes* on NBC. It talked about one of the reasons people like the show is that so many people are looking for a hero or wish that they had superpowers. Now, I definitely do not have superpowers, unless you count being able to carry in five bags of groceries on one arm with a toddler, a diaper bag, and a helium balloon on the other arm, but I do have a hero.

My dad was born on this day in 1945. He was the first-born son of my grandparents, who were themselves the children of Italian immigrants. He wasn't born into a family that had much, but what they lacked in material possessions, they more than made up for in love. Y'all have never met a group of people that are as quick to take you in, feed you a meal, hug you, and kiss you right on the mouth before you leave. My dad carries their spirit of laughter, love, and the importance of family with him to this day, and it overflows to everyone he meets.

The stories of him during childhood are legendary, including one that involves him cutting up a new straw cowboy hat because the candy counter at the movie theater was closed. He still retains a little of that temper to this day, which you'll see if you ever ride in a car with him.

He has worked hard his entire life and is a very successful man. Whenever I meet anyone who works with him, they are always quick to tell me what an incredible person they think he is and how much they respect him. I know those things about him already, but I always feel so proud to hear that about him, especially knowing that he got where he is by being a man of integrity and character.

When I was in college, I would often call him and ask him if I could take a road trip with some friends or something else that would require extra money, and he'd always say, "Well, maybe I could sell a few of my suits." It became a huge joke with all my friends, and we'd always refer to things by how many suits it was going to cost my dad. For example, my wedding probably cost his entire fall and spring wardrobe.

Speaking of wardrobe, we love to kid him about his weekend attire. For a man who is impeccably well-dressed and groomed during the week, he knows how to relax his style for the weekend. He is still the proud owner of a rust-colored velour jogging suit circa 1975, and we're not totally sure that he won't decide to pull it out and wear it. In fact, one time he was with my stepmom getting his haircut on a Saturday and a woman came up to her, not realizing she was with my dad and said, "That man would be really nice-looking if he'd just shave." He just laughs and always says, "I'm not a slave to fashion."

I've always known that he is a great father, but watching him as a grandfather with Caroline makes me love him even more. She adores her Bops, and he adores her. They are the true definition of a mutual admiration society. I always laugh because she'll ask him to do something absurd and he'll actually do it. I think she plays a little game in her head called "Let's see what Bops will do next" because she has realized there is really no limit.

So today I wish a big "Happy Birthday" to my daddy, my hero. I love you and am so proud to be your daughter. You're daily creating a rich legacy and a path that I can only hope to follow.

Sweet, right? A nice moment for a grown daughter to acknowledge her father publicly to forty-five people.

I wrote it late one night while I was at a sales meeting for my pharmaceutical job and scheduled it to publish early the next morning. I woke up and had meetings until early afternoon when I finally headed to the airport and began to check my messages. I had one from my dad asking me to call him when I had a chance, so I called him from the airport, assuming he was calling to thank me for the birthday post. He picked up on the first ring, and I said, "Happy birthday! I hope you're having a great day!" to which he responded, "Thank you. I loved your post! What you said means so much to me! But I was also calling to see if you'd read the comments."

"Not yet. Why?" I asked.

He elaborated, "Well, someone anonymously posted several rude comments, and I just wanted to make sure you were aware of it. I don't know if you can tell who left them."

I felt like I was on the verge of a panic attack. And I had an idea who had left those comments, because I'd known when I wrote the post that my mom would probably read it and be infuriated. I'd wrestled with that in the hotel room as I weighed how much I wanted to do something nice for my dad against the prospect of facing my mom's wrath. Ultimately, it was a pivotal moment for me when I decided I was done letting her intimidate me into silence, especially at the expense of people I loved. So I wrote the post with a feeling I might have to face an angry, accusatory phone call at some point down the road. However, I didn't factor in that she might choose to air all her grievances in my comments section.

I sat down at a random airport gate as soon as I hung up with my dad, and I opened my laptop to see what had been written. There were three separate comments, all left anonymously.

"Too bad people don't know who your dad really is and what he did. They wouldn't be leaving these nice comments about him."

"You didn't mention anything about your mom and that she basically had to raise you by herself."

"Your dad isn't the hero you make him out to be."

Listen, I know just enough about the internet to be dangerous. Although I was able to track that all three comments had come from the same IP address, I had no idea how to confirm that it was my mom who had left them. But I was almost sure.

I deleted the comments from the post and sat there in the airport, shocked that she would be so ugly on a public forum and also dumbfounded that she was essentially gaslighting me about the truth she'd confessed to me all those years earlier. Did she not remember what she'd told me? Did she think I wouldn't remember?

Later that night when I got home, I talked to Perry about the negative comments and felt sick that they had stayed up on my blog for most of the day. Who had seen them? What were they possibly thinking? The birthday post was supposed to be a sweet gesture to my dad and had instead turned into a hurtful situation and an attempt to embarrass him. I called my mom and could tell as soon as I heard the tone of her voice that she probably had been the one who had done this. She was short with me, and there was an edge to every word as she said, "No, I didn't do that. Maybe it was one of my friends."

Yes, maybe. Except, by this time, she lived in Oklahoma and none of her friends even knew my dad. What sane person would go on someone's child's website and leave defamatory, accusatory comments about the child's father?

And then she said, "Well, whoever left those comments was right about what they said."

That's when I knew for sure.

My voice was shaking as I responded, "Mom, you know I know the truth. And I've been married long enough now to know that it takes two people to make or break a marriage. You can't keep playing victim with me. I'm tired of it, and it's not the truth."

She replied, "Well, you're being ridiculous. I'll talk to you later when you decide to calm down." And then she hung up.

I sat there, stunned, but that moment was when I really began to think about what it would mean to cut her out of my life forever. Before that, it had always been a fleeting thought but not something I believed I could ever actually do. How do you make the decision to sever a relationship with one of your parents? The whole idea of it scared me more than I was willing to admit. What would that even look like? I also wondered if cutting my mom completely out of my life seemed *overly dramatic*—a phrase she'd used all my life to make me feel stupid whenever I voiced my feelings about anything. I didn't want to prove her right. Perhaps walking away from one of your parents was a move best reserved for a plot point in a very dramatic Lifetime movie.

But as I thought it through, I realized for the first time that *the only power she had over me was the power I gave her.* She couldn't destroy my marriage or take away Caroline. She couldn't turn my friends or other close family members against me, because they'd seen firsthand all the damage she'd done over the years. It was the most freeing thought when I let myself really begin to visualize the peace I might feel if I just closed that door.

The thing I determined that night was that our relationship felt more like a terrorist/hostage situation and that I was never going to be able to meet her demands. I'd been trying for most of my life, and I was exhausted. It was as if I'd been running in circles for years and finally realized I was going absolutely nowhere.

So I sat down at my computer and typed out a six-page letter detailing all the reasons I couldn't deal with her anymore and all the things she'd done over the years that led me to that conclusion. It was cathartic, and writing it all out made it seem even more valid.

When you live with something your whole life, you lose perspective on what's normal and what's not. I was tired of all the manipulation and anger and lies. I was tired of feeling like I was constantly at risk of making a misstep without even realizing it. I was exhausted from all the years of trying to manage my behavior or an environment to make sure my mom didn't blow it all up. God had given me this beautiful family of my own, the thing I'd prayed for most of my life, and I wanted to enjoy it in peace. I was so tired of the emotional chaos and didn't want to waste any more time dealing with it.

But I didn't send the letter.

Something in me still wanted to protect my mom from more pain in what was already a life full of hurt. I struggled with what it meant to break the chains of generational trauma and create a new legacy versus being unforgiving, bitter, and coldhearted. I knew that when and if I decided to walk away forever, it needed to be done with prayer and thought and not just as a reaction to bad behavior. And if I couldn't do it with grace and forgiveness in my heart, I was ultimately going to perpetuate a cycle that I was trying desperately to end.

CHAPTER 11

Walking Away

Over the next few years, my blog readership continued to grow and led to some opportunities that made Perry and me believe I could turn writing into a full-time job, even though we didn't know exactly what that would look like. I had a literary agent reach out to me and ask if I'd ever thought about writing a book. My friend and podcast partner, Sophie, and I were offered the opportunity to begin writing a blog for Lifeway, which meant traveling to their various women's events and then writing about them to promote interest.

Lest this sound more glamorous than it was, let me tell you that our first couple of traveling assignments with Lifeway didn't so much involve hanging out with Beth Moore and Priscilla Shirer as it did selling two-dollar T-shirts at a merch table and serving cake at an after-party event. You know what women love? A T-shirt that costs only two dollars. You know what I'm not good at? Counting change and managing a long line at a merch table. If you were at that event, there's a good chance I owe you something like nineteen cents. But we had a lot of fun and met some incredible people who still remain some of my closest friends.

I look back at those years and see where God really gave me an inside glimpse into what ministry looks like and the chance to see it done by some of the very best people with the purest of hearts. They are offstage exactly who they are onstage, and I know enough now to realize not everyone is like that.

Anyway, right before Caroline's fourth birthday, Perry and I made the decision that I should leave my pharmaceutical sales job and pursue writing full-time. It was a scary leap of faith, but the real upside for me was that I could be home with Caroline. Perry was transitioning out of his own career in youth ministry to grow the landscape business he'd started several years earlier. What I'm trying to say here is that finances were tight. As in, I have a memory of buying a fifteen-dollar jacket at Old Navy and realizing I needed to return it because we just didn't have that kind of disposable income. So, imagine my dilemma when Beth Moore called and invited me to join her and her staff on a trip to Israel. Everything about it sounded like the dream trip of a lifetime, except for the part where I would have to pay my own travel expenses. There was no way I could justify pulling money out of our meager savings to do that.

A few nights later, I was talking to my mom on the phone and casually mentioned the trip opportunity and how disappointed I was to have to turn it down. That was really all that was said, so I was shocked when she called me back a couple of nights later to tell me, "Melanie, I've been thinking about that trip, and I'd love to give you the money to go."

I've never wanted to cash a check more. But I knew deep in my heart that taking that money from her was going to come with a toll that was higher than I wanted to pay. I told her that although I so appreciated the offer, I needed to talk to Perry about it. That night over dinner, I brought up the offer my mom had made. Perry put his fork down, looked at me, and cautiously said, "I'm not going to tell you that you can't take that money. And I know how much you want to go on this trip. But you have to ask yourself if taking money from her is going to be worth the cost."

I hate when husbands confirm what you already know.

And as if I needed further reassurance that accepting the money wouldn't be the right move, the way that I dreaded calling her to say "Thanks, but no thanks" told me all I needed to know. I put it off for a couple of days before I finally called and said, "Mom, I cannot tell you how much I appreciate the financial offer. It means so much to me. But after talking it over with Perry, we agreed it just isn't the right time for me to take a trip that long while Caroline is still so young. Truly, though, thank you so much for the offer."

There was at least a minute of silence on the other end of the line, and I held my breath as I waited for how she would respond.

"Well, this is just like you," she began. "I am trying to do something nice, and you just push it back in my face."

"No, that's not it," I explained. "It really is so generous, but I don't want to leave Caroline for ten days right now—"

She interrupted me before I got to the end of my sentence and said, "I'll tell you something, Melanie. You have caused me more pain than anything else in my life."

I won't even pretend like that was a statement that didn't haunt me and make me question myself for years afterward, even though I knew it was unfair and inaccurate. She'd managed to cause herself plenty of pain by her own continued determination to throw away any chance she had for peace and happiness. It also confirmed that I was absolutely right in not taking the money from her: It wasn't about her desire to see me take this trip of a lifetime as much as it was a way for her to regain some control over me that she'd lost as I grew healthier and set more boundaries in our relationship to protect myself, my child, and my marriage.

Also, I still haven't made it to Israel. Maybe I can put that on my schedule now that my baby is twenty and in college. And I'll buy myself a fifteen-dollar Old Navy jacket to take with me.

· · · · · ·

There are a few people I can't imagine living without. They are my true blues. My ride or dies. The people who would hide a body if I asked them to. Not that I would ever need a body hidden, but I'm just trying to emphasize their loyalty in a dramatic fashion. Gulley is one of those people for me. She and I have lived just a mile apart for the past twenty years, and I can't tell you what a gift it was to get to raise our kids together. The days that one of us would call the other in desperation and say, "Help! We have got to get out of the house and burn some energy," are too many to count. We spent endless summer days at the neighborhood pool, letting the kids wear themselves out by intermittently jumping off the diving board and seeing who could touch the bottom of the deep end. There were days when we'd just set them loose in Gulley's huge backyard and watch them speed around in her son Jackson's little battery-operated Jeep, usually while taking turns towing one another behind it in a little red wagon. If I heard Gulley yell once, "What are you doing? Do you want to end up in the emergency room?" I heard her yell it a thousand times over the years. Man, we had a lot of fun.

But one of the best things we ever did was take road trips together. Gulley's parents, Honey and Big, live in Bryan, Texas, about a three-hour drive from San Antonio. We started going to see them when the kids were all little enough that at least one of them was still in a rear-facing car seat. We have the best memories from those trips, even though, at the time, they often seemed like an endless montage of someone eating too much candy, someone throwing up, and someone crying that we were playing the music too loud.

During spring break of 2010, Caroline was in first grade. Gulley and I decided that our best vacation option would be to go on a road trip to Honey and Big's and spend part of the week taking the kids to watch the Aggies play baseball. And then Caroline and I planned to leave Bryan a few days early and meet Mimi and Bops in Houston because Caroline had big dreams of getting to ice-skate at the Galleria.

I talked to my mom on the phone a few days before we left and told her our plans, although I left out the part about driving to Houston to meet Mimi and Bops. I knew it would just set her off, and we were operating in what I thought was a pretty good place at the moment. My sister had given birth to her son, Luke, back in December, so I'd done for her what she'd done for me and run interference with my mom so Amy could relax. Mom even stayed at my house for a couple of nights, and we'd had what I thought were some good talks about life and motherhood. We laughed a lot, and for the first time in a long time,

I felt pretty good about our relationship and believed maybe we'd finally landed in a place that felt comfortable for both of us. During the months after that, we'd talked on the phone more. So much of the tension and anger that were always right under the surface seemed to have dissipated. I wasn't sure what had changed, but I was grateful for the peace it brought, even though something inside me kept warning me that history had proved the other shoe could drop at any given moment.

So that's why when I woke up at Honey's house on Wednesday morning of spring break and saw that I had a missed call and a message from my mom that she'd left at 7:30 A.M., I knew in my heart it wasn't going to be good. In fact, I waited about thirty minutes before I listened to it because I had a sick feeling in the pit of my stomach and wanted to delay what I felt certain was coming. I'd written about our road trip and posted it on the blog late the night before, and I had a feeling that reading about our good time had set her off. I finished my first cup of coffee and then went into my bedroom to listen to her message by myself.

As soon as I hit play, I heard, "Melanie, I just read about your little trip. And I can't believe that you are only thirty minutes away from your grandmother and aren't taking the time to go visit her. I have had it with you. You are so damn selfish. I am so damn sick of you, and if me saying that to you is the end of our relationship forever, then so be it."

I'd been waiting for the other shoe to drop, and there it came flying through the phone and hitting me squarely in the side of the head. It was a textbook move for her to find any reason to lash out at me without giving me any notice or a chance to explain anything. If she could still be this venomous and mean despite the past few months of mending pieces of our relationship, then I didn't see any way forward. I just felt broken. I don't know if I knew it for sure at that moment, but her voicing that she was fine with ending our relationship finally set me free to walk away.

I'd been a mom for only six years, but I knew with everything in me that there would never be anything Caroline could say or do that would make me threaten to end my relationship with her. My own motherhood gave me an insight that I'd been missing prior to having my own child. It confirmed what I'd known since that first week I brought Caroline home from the hospital: My mom didn't love me like I loved my daughter. I don't even think it's that she didn't so much as she couldn't. Something inside her wasn't healthy enough to love anyone without constantly sabotaging the relationship.

I would be lying if I said her words didn't hurt. There was something about realizing she'd still been harboring all this unspoken resentment toward me that was more than I could bear. In that moment, I realized I would never be safe in the relationship and could never really be healed and whole with my mom in my life. Caroline and I got in the car and headed to Houston to meet Mimi and Bops as planned, but I cried the whole way there. I was so angry that this fun trip I'd planned with Caroline was just one more thing that my mom had come in and wrecked.

I pulled myself together and made it through the rest of that week, pretending everything was fine despite feeling shattered. My mom called me repeatedly and left voicemails telling me that she hadn't meant what she'd said but that it was also my fault for making her so angry.

I prayed about the situation over the next several weeks, desperately wanting to handle it the way I believed God was leading me. I was confident He was telling me I was free to walk away.

So I did.

CHAPTER 12

Cutting Off the Source
of the Pain

One thing I've learned in life is that it's sweeter with a dog. There is something about the unconditional love a pup offers that speaks to my soul. I believe a dog can teach us valuable lessons about what it means to love our people, and recently God used our dog Piper to show me something profound.

When Caroline was ten years old, we participated in the time-honored tradition of getting a puppy. Actually, we ended up with two puppies because moderation has never really been our strong suit. Perry, in particular, lives by the motto "If one is good, then 145 are better." Despite already having two elderly dogs at home, we thought it was time for Caroline to finally have the puppy she'd always wanted. That is how we ended up with two Blue Lacy puppies named Piper and Mabel.

Mabel and I have been each other's emotional support animal since the day we brought her home and I realized she's a little high-strung and anxious, as evidenced by the fact she threw up the entire car ride home. That was really all it took for me to decide that I would hold her close forever to quell all her fears and nervous energy. Stay tuned for my next book, *Co-dependency: A Dog Love Story*.

Meanwhile, Piper was Caroline's dog from day one. The two of them were inseparable, and Piper followed her everywhere. She slept in her room every night and rode with me to each soccer practice and school pickup line with her eyes roaming about until she found her girl and began to jump and buck excitedly like a horse at a rodeo. To this day, when I get a call and Piper hears Caroline's ringtone, she runs to the back door and is ready to go pick her up. She's the best, most loyal girl.

But about two years ago, we discovered a small lump on Piper's front left paw that seemed to be growing larger. We took her to the vet to have it biopsied, and that's when we found out Piper had contracted a rare fungal infection in her paw. We have no idea how or when it happened; we just know that it had begun to invade all her soft tissue. Our vet, Dr. Alldredge, removed what she could but warned us it would probably come back. Sure enough, over the next six months, we watched as Piper's paw pad and the top of her paw became increasingly swollen. We visited several specialists to see if anyone had any suggestions as to how to treat it but kept getting the same answer: The only real solution was going to be to amputate her leg. Amputation seemed so extreme, so we decided to wait and just see what happened over the next year or so. We wanted to do only what was best for Piper, and it's hard to do that when your dog can't look at you and just say, "Hey, why don't we go ahead and cut off this leg?"

Then about a month ago, we realized that Piper's paw was getting worse. It had become so inflamed and swollen that you could tell it was a matter of time before the whole paw would split open and cause potentially even more problems in terms of infection. Perry and I knew it was time to pursue getting the leg amputated, especially considering that Piper was otherwise in perfect health. After a thorough examination to make sure Piper was a good candidate for amputation, Dr. Alldredge concurred that it was time for her to lose the diseased leg. We scheduled the surgery, I cried when we dropped her off, and Dr. Alldredge sent us a video about four hours later of Piper walking around on three legs post-surgery as if she'd been doing it forever.

Watching Piper recover that quickly from something so traumatic has been remarkable. Dr. Alldredge said it's probably due largely to the fact that she'd been compensating for that diseased paw for a long time and that it might have been causing her more pain and discomfort than any of us realized until it was gone. We'd tried every way we could think of to avoid the amputation because it seemed so extreme, but no amount of surface healing could fix the disease that had become so deeply embedded.

And what hit me as we watched Piper recover so completely is that *sometimes true healing can't take place until you cut off the source of the pain.*

So, that's a sermon in the form of a dog's amputation.

The months after I made the decision to cut my mom out of my life weren't easy, as I often second-guessed myself and wondered if I were being too harsh. And the bond between a parent and child is meant to be one that isn't easy to sever without a second thought.

Over the years, I've told so many people in similar situations that there is no way you can make that kind of decision and say,

"Man, it feels great to have no contact with my mother." It's not how we're designed, and I grieved that loss deeply. But I also knew way down in my soul that it was the right thing to do. God was so faithful to confirm that for me anytime I began to question what I'd done or think about opening that door again. He kept leading me to Matthew 7:16–20:

> By their fruit you will recognize them. Do people pick grapes from thornbushes, or figs from thistles? Likewise, every good tree bears good fruit, but a bad tree bears bad fruit. A good tree cannot bear bad fruit, and a bad tree cannot bear good fruit. Every tree that does not bear good fruit is cut down and thrown into the fire. Thus, by their fruit you will recognize them.

When I looked at my mom's life and, more specifically, at the emotional wake she constantly left behind her, it was evident that she was a branch in my life that needed to be removed. And the most difficult part in coming to that conclusion was there had been some good fruit in terms of her influence on me, but her mental state had devolved to the point where it seemed that all she could produce was bad fruit. Proverbs 14:30 says, "A heart at peace gives life to the body, but envy rots the bones," and I believe with everything in me that all the years of bitterness and unforgiveness had taken their toll on Mom. That was yet another pattern I didn't want to perpetuate in my own life, so I continually prayed for peace to fully forgive her. And I also prayed that God would make it clear if that relationship was a door I needed to reopen at some point.

However, the more distance I got from my mom, the more

I realized how destructive some of her behavior patterns had been to her and those around her. It took me years to realize that so many things I'd grown up believing to be normal weren't the way healthy mother-daughter interactions should work.

A wise friend once told me, "Sometimes the Enemy puts crazy so close to you to make you believe you're the one who's crazy." This summed up so much of what I'd wrestled with most of my life. I always felt like I was the problem. *If I could just be good enough, if I could just be what my mom needs me to be, if I could just quit saying the wrong thing*—the list was endless. I spent so many years believing that maybe I was the one who was selfish, damaged, and inflicting pain on the people around me, because that's what she'd always told me. But then God was so faithful to direct me to all the other relationships I have that are healthy and whole. My friendships, my marriage, and my relationship with Caroline were the guideposts that brought me much-needed assurance that I was able to develop and maintain fruitful connections.

And I needed that reassurance because Suzanne spent the years after I cut off communication leading a full-scale PR campaign against me. She called Amy and said, "I can't believe Melanie has done this. I can't think of one single thing I've ever done that would make her do this." She left messages for Gulley, my mother-in-law, my dad, and Perry. At one point, she even told Amy, "I feel bad for Perry. I know he really likes me, and I'm sure he thinks Melanie is wrong for doing this. She's always been so selfish." She left comments on my blog, she emailed various acquaintances of mine I knew through other blogs, she posted on my Facebook page, and in a move that still astounds me to this day, she even called Beth Moore's office and said she would like to talk to Beth about me. I received letters from women from her church I'd never even met who told me how wrong I was to abandon my mother and that I needed to let my mom back into my life because it's what God would want. And when I went to visit Nanny at her assisted-living home about six months into the whole thing, she took my hand and said, "Melanie, enough of this foolishness. You need to talk to your mom. The Bible says even a whore honors her mother."

Does it, though?

Also, am I the whore in this scenario?

But ironically, Suzanne never attempted to reach out to me personally. She had my email, my phone number, and my address. But instead of trying to contact me directly, she repeatedly chose to contact only people around me, and in a very public way. It highlighted what I already knew: This wasn't about me at all; it was about her not getting her way and wanting to shame me for it. One of the truest things I've ever heard is that the people in your life who require you to set boundaries are the very ones who will rail the hardest against any line you draw. And I'd drawn the hardest line of my life.

As for me, the more time that passed, the more at peace I felt. I'd spent so many years trying to twist myself into some version of what I thought might keep Suzanne calm, hoping and praying this or that circumstance would be the thing that would bring her contentment or make her change. I was suddenly free from that pressure. The thing I'd prayed for since the moment I found out I was having a daughter was that God would give me guidance and do whatever needed to be done in my own life so I could raise Caroline to be emotionally and spiritually healthy.

But you can't lead someone to a place that's beyond where you've been able to go yourself. If I truly wanted to break this generational cycle that perpetuated a mean-girl culture, I had to fully feel the pain of it and give myself space to heal. Being free of Suzanne was finally allowing the deepest parts of me to become whole. I accepted that she was most likely never going to change and that it wasn't my job to try to make her do so. I was able to concentrate on Caroline and my family without having to constantly navigate everything with my mom. I was living out Isaiah 44:3, the verse God had given me when I was pregnant with Caroline, and watching Him "pour water on the thirsty land, and streams on the dry ground."

From the time Caroline was born, all I wanted was for the two of us to have a healthy, close relationship. I wanted her to know she could always count on me to be her number one supporter. I never wanted her to feel as though she had to dim her light to make me or anyone else feel better. I never wanted her to feel like she was responsible for my emotional well-being. I wanted to raise her to be strong and secure and to know her worth in any and every situation. I wanted her to find the purpose and joy in loving the people around her instead of getting caught up in the trap of comparing herself with others. I tried to instill in her that life is better when you focus on the people and things in your life that are good and true and that it's okay to walk away from people who want to tear you down. There is no opportunity and no relationship that is worth being anything less than what God created you to be.

But I had to work to become that person myself by allowing

God to heal what was broken in my life before He could equip me to teach Caroline to be all those things.

I remember one Sunday at church not long after I'd realized I could no longer have my mom in my life when our pastor, Sean Azzaro, preached a sermon on forgiveness and said, "You can have forgiveness without reconciliation or restoration of the relationship." It hit me way down deep because what I'd begun to realize as I had time to step back from this toxic relationship and heal was that I truly didn't harbor any bitterness, resentment, or unforgiveness toward my mom. Bitterness and anger were part of the cycle I was trying to break. I wanted to be sure that in making this decision, I wasn't perpetuating those very things. It was about breaking a cycle, not creating a new, equally destructive one.

As I mothered Caroline, I grieved for the younger version of myself who missed out on having a mom who was able to love me in a healthy, supportive way. However, the key to letting God completely heal you is to fully grieve as you surrender the hope you had that things could be different and trust that He will redeem what you've been through in ways you can't see at the time. He will truly give us beauty for the ashes of things in our lives that have burned down.

I knew that everything my mom had done and said had been out of her own woundedness and brokenness, and I could look at her life and see the choices and events that had caused much of that. It made me sad for her. Could she have been capable of more? Absolutely. Did she choose that path? No.

I didn't understand it, but I forgave it. Only God could have given me such a spirit of tenderness toward my mom in order for me to forgive her. But He also gave me the clarity to know that the only way for me to really heal was to cut off a relation-ship that had become too diseased to ever be healthy.

Amputation is a hard decision to make. But there are times when the only way forward is to cut off the very thing making you sick.

CHAPTER 13

Healing Below the Surface

We live in the same neighborhood where Perry grew up and his parents were raised. What I'm saying is that his roots are deep in this community. When Caroline started school, it was always funny when we'd attend a back-to-school night or other school function because it pretty much turned into an impromptu high school reunion for Perry. The times he would see a kid and say, "That has to be John Smith's daughter. Looks just like him," and he turned out to be correct are infinite. DNA is a powerful thing. And we hand down more than just blue eyes and a crooked smile.

When Caroline was in sixth grade, Perry decided to run for a position on our local school board and ended up serving there for six years. It gave him an inside view to various issues within our neighborhood. One of the biggest challenges was the constant struggle to navigate the alcohol and drug use among the high school students.

A large part of the problem was that many parents felt it was no big deal to provide alcohol to minors in their home or rent party buses for the teens and ignore all the vodka and tequila bottles that made their way onto the buses. Did I first hear the phrase "a handle of vodka" from a sophomore girl? Yes. Yes, I did. There are many parents who are the embodiment of Amy Poehler in *Mean Girls:* "I'm not like a regular mom; I'm a cool mom."[1] I know high school kids are going to drink; I'm just not cool enough to think we should enable them to do it. I believe if kids are going to drink, they should at least do it without their parents' knowledge and the way we all did it in the eighties: Find a seedy convenience store on the wrong side of town that will turn a blind eye to their purchase of a couple of bottles of Zima as opposed to their parents supplying them with top-shelf alcohol.

One specific conversation we had really opened my eyes to the things we can inadvertently hand down to our children, believing them to be harmless in the name of "It's not that big a deal" or justifying that it's the way our parents did things.

After a school board meeting where this problem was addressed after yet another school event where a bunch of kids got in trouble for being drunk, Perry came home and said, "Here's the thing that breaks my heart. When you read the names of the kids on these lists who have gotten caught drinking or shown up drunk to a school function, I know those names. I grew up with many of their parents. It's more than just harmless drinking; it's a generational pattern of creating alcoholics. And it's all being justified or ignored with the rationale that it's how *they* were raised and they turned out fine. But why do you want to open your child's life to something that could ultimately destroy them?"

Here's where I want to pause to tell you that Perry and I both drink on occasion and my point isn't about alcohol itself. Instead, it's about allowing what have been destructive generational patterns to continue unchecked. These issues can take so many forms.

A while back, I was reading through the Bible in a year, which led me to Numbers 13. In that chapter, after Moses led the children of Israel out of slavery, after they saw the Red Sea part as they escaped Pharaoh, and after God provided for them time and time again, we see them reach the edge of the land God promised them. Moses sent spies into the land to find out more about it.

> See what the land is like and whether the people who live there are strong or weak, few or many. What kind of land do they live in? Is it good or bad? What kind of towns do they live in? Are they unwalled or fortified? How is the soil? Is it fertile or poor? Are there trees in it or not? Do your best to bring back some of the fruit of the land. (verses 18–20)

God had instructed Moses to send twelve men, twelve leaders, to go investigate the land He had for them, and only two, Joshua and Caleb, came back believing they could take the land. The other ten saw only the obstacles and all the reasons the plan wouldn't work. Verses 31–33 tell us their mindset:

> "We can't attack those people; they are stronger than we are." And they spread among the Israelites a bad report about the land they had explored. They said, "The land we explored devours those living in it. All the people we saw there are of great size. We saw the Nephilim there (the descendants of

Anak come from the Nephilim). We seemed like grasshoppers in our own eyes, and we looked the same to them."

They saw the obstacles, lost sight of the faithfulness of God, and let their fear take over. It was their land, but they had to be brave enough to take it. The same is true for you. To take hold of the new and leave behind the old, you have to face your fears and let go of the destructive attitude that wants to hold you in the very place you are being called to leave. And here's the thing: There will be people in your life who want to keep you imprisoned in what you are trying to leave behind, because that's what feels familiar and safe to them.

We watch the Israelites as fear prevailed and took over the entire camp. By that night, they were completely freaking out and had totally lost sight of all the ways God delivered them over and over. God saw their disbelief, their unwillingness to trust in His provision and protection, and vowed that none of their generation would enter the Promised Land except for Caleb and Joshua.

In what wasn't a coincidence, ten of the twelve leaders didn't even mention God as they discussed what they'd seen, choosing to focus solely on what terrified them about the new land. Joshua and Caleb had seen the same giants and the same heavily fortified cities, but they were looking through the lens of faith. They believed that God wouldn't have brought them this far only to leave them now. Meanwhile, the others were literally holding the fruit of the land in their hands while doubting God and wishing they could just go back to Egypt even though that meant being enslaved again—the very thing they'd spent all this time trying to escape. And ultimately, because of their parents' unbelief, the younger generation of Israelites ended up having to wander in the desert for forty more years.

I don't think any of us want that for our kids. We don't want to see them suffer for the places where we have failed or fallen into destructive patterns. But how do we prevent it? How do we stop the cycles of destruction that get passed down like some terrible hand-me-downs that no one really wants?

There are patterns that become so ingrained in a family line that they seem normal to us until our eyes are opened to the truth. And then we have to be willing to deal with those patterns even when the people around us want to make it seem as though *we* are the ones being unfair or extreme.

I knew for most of my life that I didn't come from a normal, healthy family dynamic. It also took me more than thirty years to realize how toxic some of the behavior patterns were and the ways that I could inadvertently hand them down unless I prayed for wisdom on how to stop the cycle. My family history, even long before my mom was born, is full of mental illness, addiction, vanity, lies, selfishness, and deception. If we didn't ask God to redeem and heal it all, those things had the ability to continue to embed themselves in the healthy family Perry and I desperately wanted to create.

When God looks at us, He also sees our family line. He sees where we came from. He sees those who came before us, and He sees those who will come long after we are gone. When God made a covenant with Abraham in Genesis, He didn't say He would bless just Abraham; He referred to blessing Abraham and his descendants (12:1–3). In God's eyes, they are one and the same. Because Abraham obeyed God, he and his descendants were blessed. Blessings run through bloodlines. But so do generational sin and trauma.

A couple of years ago, I watched the movie *Redeeming Love,* based on the book by Francine Rivers, and a line has stayed with me: "You have to leave behind what you were born into to become who God meant you to be."[2] But that is so much easier said than done.

We all have an inner leaning to repeat the patterns that run in our families. And we might be able to mask these tendencies for years before some circumstance causes them to rise to the surface and cause real problems. Unless you deal with the root of any issue, it's always going to repeat itself in some way. This goes back to Perry's delicate saying, "If you don't deal with your sh%$, it's going to come out sideways," or, as Lamentations 5:7 says, "Our ancestors sinned and are no more, and we bear their punishment."

So, even though those family members may be long gone, the effects of the sins they carried can stick with us if we don't allow Jesus to heal those places. We have to make the decision to break destructive patterns that we don't want to continue to hand down. And the effects of generational sin take so many forms: disease, divorce, abuse, violence, alcoholism, drug addiction, adultery, mental illness, anxiety, fear, and the need to control everything. Basically, a laundry list of things that fall into the category of Not Great, Bob.

Whatever the things that run through bloodlines, it takes only one brave person to decide the cycle ends here. When you look at your family's history and see behavior that you don't want to repeat, God will give you the strength to break those chains if you ask Him. This is about the redemptive blood of Jesus Christ. In 1 Peter 1:18–19, we read, "You know that it was not with perishable things such as silver or gold that you were redeemed from the empty way of life handed down to you from your ancestors, but with the precious blood of Christ, a lamb without blemish or defect."

Because I've already confessed to you that vanity runs deep in my family, I'm going to tell you about my face. Once I hit my fifties, a lot of humbling physical changes came along with that milestone. In particular, all the years I'd spent lying out in the sun showed up across my face in the form of dark splotches and wrinkles. These are the things you think won't happen to you when you're nineteen and have a tan that could put you on a Coppertone billboard. But as it turns out, you need to wear sunscreen every day, children. Preferably SPF 165.

So, thanks to all this sun damage, I now go see a lovely skin aesthetician named Niva once a month. Niva is essentially a face artist who tells me what treatments I need to do to make my face look better, and I do exactly what she tells me. But because I'm a scientist at heart, I'm always doing my own research in the form of watching videos from Instagram influencers to discover any potential new treatments that will help me look ten years younger. That is why, a few weeks ago, I walked into Niva's clinic and said, "Tell me about Halo laser treatment. Should I do that?" Niva looked at my face carefully as she explained, "You could do Halo, but it's a pretty painful treatment because it goes way below the surface to heal all the damage that's been done over the years. It just depends on if you want to make your skin look better on the surface or if you want to address all the underlying causes of the damage."

And while she was still talking, I realized that what she was saying was so profound when you think about it in terms of generational cycles. It's always painful to heal all the things that lie beneath the surface because it means you have to acknowledge the root cause of the trauma. We are masters at making things look better on the surface, but when we decide we really want to heal the deepest parts of ourselves, a lot more work and a lot more pain are required as we break away from people and things that once felt comfortable to us.

It's often the wounds caused by our families that cut the deepest and leave the most apparent scars, but God can absolutely heal those wounds. Your family history doesn't have to be your future. Ask Him to stop the dysfunction and create a new legacy, and then watch what He does. He is the road map that will guide you into a new land of promise and freedom if you trust Him enough to walk that path in obedience.

Generational sin is no match for the power and peace we can find in Christ if we are brave enough to create something new. Beth Moore once told me in a conversation we had about my mom, "Melanie, there are some fields in your life where God just shows you that field is dead. You realize there is nothing for you anymore and walk away."

And I found that very thought echoed in Isaiah 43:19:

See, I am doing a new thing!
Now it springs up; do you not perceive it?
I am making a way in the wilderness
and streams in the wasteland.

God specializes in taking the places in our lives that feel barren and doing something refreshing, healing, and new.

When Perry and I got married at the tender age of twenty-six—full of all the bravado, swagger, and confidence of two young, dumb people who don't know any better—we had no inkling of how hard the road would often be to create a new family legacy. But we also had no idea how faithful God would be to guide us every step of the way and give us the wisdom to make hard decisions. I certainly didn't anticipate that it would lead to the drastic step of walking away from my mom. However, as hard as it was, I couldn't have envisioned at that point in my life how important my spiritual and emotional health was going to be as I guided Caroline through her teen years.

But I was about to find out.

CHAPTER 14

You Can't Sit at Our Table

As we went through Caroline's elementary school years and even junior high, I often breathed a sigh of relief that they hadn't been as hard as I thought they might have been. I mean, sure there was the weird dynamic of having to tell her teachers and the front office staff that if my mom ever came to pick Caroline up from school, they were under no circumstances to allow Caroline to leave with her. It probably didn't help that I always felt a need to overexplain the situation in a way that made everyone involved feel slightly uncomfortable, but that is who I am. My gift is not so much small talk but rather just diving straight into the deep end and telling you my entire life story—including all my hopes and worries—within the first ten minutes of our conversation. I'm like George Costanza from *Seinfeld:* "That's it. All of my darkest fears and everything I'm capable of. That's me."[1] ("Also, what was your name again?")

Anyway, Caroline was a happy kid with a fun personality and usually managed to find her way. She comes at the world with a boldness I've always kind of marveled over because it's so dif-

ferent from how I operate. She has never been afraid to advocate for herself in social settings and has always been up for
meeting new people and experiencing new things. She's also
always had insight beyond her years in different situations.

When she was in third grade, we were invited to a party at
our local country club. It was an over-the-top extravaganza
with face painters and rides and clowns making balloon animals on demand. I remember thinking that it was going to ruin
her for all other party experiences because nothing in our normally average life could ever top it. But as we picked up our car
from valet parking, she said, "I don't really think these are our
kind of people." And I recognized that she understood something that had taken me most of my life to figure out when I
found myself among social dynamics that weren't really my
thing.

But I paid attention to her friendships throughout her childhood and coached her to be better when it felt like she needed
to be kinder or have more understanding and empathy. I saw
that other kids liked her, and she always had a few close friends
that we had over for regular playdates and all that, because she
is a child of the 2000s and parents arrange playdates now. Back
in the seventies, a playdate was when your parents kicked you
out of the house for the day and told you they didn't want to see
you until the streetlights came on.

Caroline was also so fortunate to have the same wonderful
teacher for three years in elementary school, a young woman
who really fostered kindness among her students, and that gave
Caroline a close-knit group of friends who cheered one another
on during those early years. Of course, then I spent time worrying about middle school because, well, middle school. It seems

like the social undercurrents really begin to change once everyone becomes more aware of all the intangible things that make
one set of kids cool and another set of kids decidedly uncool.
There's a reason you rarely hear anyone say, "You know what
years of my life I loved? Middle school."

I still remember vividly the first week of middle school when
Caroline came home and told me that a girl who had been her
friend since the earliest days of childhood basically ignored her
in class. I tried to explain that it wasn't a reflection on Caroline
but just that this girl may be feeling insecure and trying to fit in
with a new group. On the inside, it made me feel so hurt and
angry on her behalf, but I did my best to be the grown-up and
help Caroline process it in a mature way. However, a few months
later, I experienced it for myself when we attended a mother-
daughter tea for an organization we'd joined because I'm an
idiot and bought into the sales pitch of "Everybody is doing
this, and it will ensure your child's admission to the college of
her choice."

Caroline and I arrived at the tea and sat at a table where we
knew practically no one, and I just had the ick feeling you get
when you don't belong and are a fish out of water. But I put on
a brave face for Caroline. When this same childhood friend
walked in with her mother, I stood up to say hello and invited
them to sit at our table. And they did. For about three minutes,
until they saw what was apparently a more desirable group to
sit with and got up and moved. I felt like I'd been punched.

On the way home, I tried to put on a bright, cheery act to
distract Caroline from what had happened. But she'd seen it.
She'd been living that out for months in the halls at school. Yes,
it hurt my feelings, but it was infinitely worse to see how it

wounded my daughter, who had loved this girl like a sister. Those are the times when you know that all the things you could say to try to brush it off wouldn't make the betrayal feel any better. I'd been prepared for Caroline's friendships to maybe ebb and flow, but I hadn't realized how that was going to shift the dynamics of some of my own friendships.

Even though it was rude behavior, it wasn't necessarily overtly mean, which made it even more difficult to know how or even if I should address it. I tried my best to help Caroline under-stand that it was part of being that age, with all the raging hor-mones and people figuring out social standings and wanting to move up the ladder. It's not right, it's not kind, but it is what it is.

There were definitely hard times, but overall it felt like by the time Caroline made it through her middle school years, she had fared pretty well and developed new friendships that I thought could stand the test of time. I'd met some other moms, and it seemed like many of us were on the same page about how we expected our girls to treat one another and the world in general.

Although we agreed in theory, in reality some kids were being left out or ignored. And unless it's your child feeling this way, it's easy to be completely unaware of or overlook the situ-ation. I know there was a time I was guilty of that as a parent.

And then it was time for high school. Man, I was about to have a complete shift of perspective. I'm not sure what I thought the high school years might bring, because I was so focused on the fact that it meant we had only four more years before Caro-line left for college, and everyone had prepared me that those years would go by in the blink of an eye. I wasn't naïve enough to think there wouldn't be bumps along the way, but I also wanted to embrace all the moments and get every bit of joy out of those last years with her at home.

As her freshman year began, I watched Caroline's friendships shift a little, but it was primarily for the better. Our high school was mostly made up of the same kids that had gone to school together since kindergarten, but there were always several private-school kids who made the switch to public school as ninth grade began. It was also a time when kids started to have more freedom to get involved with different clubs and teams, which ideally would help them find their place. All I wanted was for Caroline to have a good group of friends. I'd prayed for this since she was young because I knew how much friends will influence the decisions you make, what you value, and how you see the world.

I think this desire was magnified for me because Caroline is an only child. I wanted her to have close girlfriends who could feel like sisters—a group that would support and encourage one another as they made their way through high school. But I have a tendency to view everything through a nostalgic lens, as though life is an episode of *The Wonder Years*. I forget that teen friendships can be complex as everyone struggles to figure out where they fit in and social hierarchy becomes its own kind of dangerous animal.

All that to say, it felt like a dream come true when Caroline got home from school one day in mid-September of ninth grade and announced that she wanted to invite a whole group of girls over before the homecoming dance in a few weeks. Plus, several of them had arranged a shopping day to go pick out their dresses together. I was all in for every bit of this because it was what I'd hoped and prayed would happen. She had a group!

And they all wanted to come to our house before the dance to get ready! This meant I could help with everyone's hair and makeup and host a fun get-together, which is basically the Venn diagram of my personality.

After weeks of planning and shopping, homecoming arrived. And let's have a moment of silence here for all the moms who have sat on the floor of a dressing room in Dillard's and prayed for death's sweet embrace as every single dress you have chosen gets dismissed like a bad singer on *American Idol*. I believe department-store dressing rooms with teenage girls are found at the intersection of desperation and lowered dress-code standards, which explains why a lot of homecoming photos look like the girls are wearing swimsuits from the 1920s.

Nevertheless, the girls all went to the football game together on Friday night, and then on Saturday they gathered at our house to get ready and eat dinner before they headed to the dance. I curled hair and helped put on eyeliner as I listened to them all laugh and talk while they moved as a unit from Caroline's bedroom to the kitchen and then to the bathroom for one final check in the mirror with the grace of giraffes wearing new high heels.

I could hear them talking about who they liked and what boy they hoped to dance with as they stopped occasionally to tell one another how beautiful they looked and how perfectly their hair was curled or their makeup was done. It just felt like everything I'd wanted Caroline to experience. Every girl was darling and polite as they thanked Perry and me for the food and for having them over. And in my mind, I was congratulating myself on this sweet group of friends Caroline was going to have for the rest of her life.

As I dropped them off at the dance and they all piled out of my car in a cloud of laughter and perfume, I told them to have the best time and drove off with tears in my eyes. I remember thinking that those were the good old days they would look back on, and I felt so incredibly blessed that Caroline had this great group of girls to make fun memories with.

And the rest of freshman year, while it had the normal ups and downs, was good. It was filled with sleepovers and shopping trips and coffee-shop outings because today's fourteen-year-olds are coffee connoisseurs as if they were raised by Juan Valdez. I had all these girls in our home multiple times over the course of that year and always did what I could to make them feel loved and supported. I made them cookies, helped with school projects, drove them home from school when they needed rides, and listened when they needed to talk out problems. I wanted our house to always be a safe, warm haven, because I knew from my own childhood years that there are kids who need that even if you can't see it from the outside.

And I felt so much peace as God continued to heal the places where I'd always felt raw. I was discovering so much redemption and beauty for ashes through my relationship with Caroline. I treasured our closeness during her teen years, when I'd been prepared for her to want to pull away. I saw the way God was using my own difficult relationship with my mom to equip me to be the mom I always wished I'd had. There is something incredibly healing about getting to be the thing in someone else's life that you wished you'd had in your own.

Maybe it's because my own high school days were far enough behind me that any drama was a distant memory, but I wasn't prepared at all for the storm that was on the horizon as Caroline began her sophomore year of high school. It came in like a lion and went out like an even meaner lion. Let's just say that even now, all these years later, if we are talking about anything that is really unpleasant, we refer to it as "sophomore year."

By the end of ninth grade, it felt like Caroline had really settled in with this group of girls who had been together since the beginning of the school year. They weren't the most popular girls in school, which felt safe to me because it seemed as though a group of semi-awkward smart girls might be a better bet. I'd watched *Mean Girls* enough times to know we wanted to avoid the Regina Georges of the world. And I'd always known that Caroline was never going to be one to have a huge tribe, because, like me, she has always preferred a handful of close friends over a large group. This handful of girls seemed to be big enough that no one was left out yet small enough to have genuine connections. Plus, I felt like I knew them, and that gave me peace of mind as a mom.

Caroline walked into her sophomore year, and I think we were both full of optimism for what tenth grade would hold. She was a varsity soccer player, she'd just gotten her braces off, her grades were excellent, and she seemed to have a pretty good sense of who she was and what she wanted. And life was pretty great until October arrived and everything began to fall apart. She would come home from school, and I could tell she felt a little uneasy as girls in the group seemed to be splitting into separate factions. Then I think there was some jealousy over a boy a few of them liked, which was pitting them against one another. I would tell you all the ins and outs of what happened there, but I'm still not entirely sure.

There were so many moving parts and different stories at

play that it was hard to make sense of what exactly was going on. But the bottom line was that Caroline's friends, over the course of a couple of weeks, completely turned against her and decided to make her life miserable with little to no warning. There was one girl in particular—ironically a girl Caroline had brought into the group because she seemed lonely—who became relentless in what seemed like a quest to ruin Caroline's life. She constantly threatened Caroline and sent her nuclear texts over the ensuing months where she promised to tell whatever lies she had to tell to make that happen.

Caroline was devastated. And beyond that, she was so confused as to why any of this was happening. She would come home after school and tell me about everything that had gone on that day, and I could just see how broken she was by this betrayal by girls she'd trusted. Caroline again asked the girls if they could all just get together and talk about what happened as she tried to figure out why they'd all turned on her. They refused. They had no interest in trying to make anything better. They just completely shut her out.

I was stunned.

I knew these girls. They'd been in our home. I'd loved them and welcomed them in. I'd put on their mascara. I'd curled their hair. I'd let them eat my Häagen-Dazs chocolate-and-peanut-butter ice cream.

A few weeks later, Caroline discovered that two of the other girls who were still pretending to be her friends were texting horrible lies about her behind her back. They'd accidentally included her in a group text she was never meant to see. A text that basically laid out their plan to destroy her socially and pointed out every flaw they could find.

Needless to say, it was awful. I felt so completely powerless. I could listen, I could try to pick up the broken pieces, but I couldn't make those other girls behave like humans instead of wolves circling wounded prey. As the girls constantly looked for ways to tear Caroline down and pick apart everything about her, I was watching her deal with so much of the same mean-girl behavior I'd experienced with my mom.

Every morning as I drove Caroline to school, I would feel sick to my stomach as I watched her try to put on a brave face for whatever she might face once she arrived. And every afternoon after I picked her up, I would listen as she told me about the latest development and what unkind things had been said or done that day, and there would usually be tears. I questioned her about her role in all of it because I wanted to make sure she hadn't done something to cause the drama. But she was as confused as I was. The thing about Caroline is she has never been afraid to have the hard conversation and speak what's on her mind, but those aren't generally traits that translate well to the high school years, when girls are content to create drama out of nothing. Caroline asked the girls repeatedly if they could all sit down and talk to work things out, but they weren't interested in that; they were only interested in continuing to keep things stirred up.

It was heartbreaking to watch my happy, secure girl become a shell of herself as she was told things like "The world would be better off without you" and "Maybe you should just kill yourself." She told us that the ringleader of the group, the girl she'd brought in, had begun following her into the bathroom at school only to continue to torment her and say things like "You're just an anorexic whore who should die."

I began to wonder if the loving words she heard inside the

walls of our home would be enough to combat what she was being told in the hallways of school and through text messages. I lived in fear that she might decide that the world would be better off without her and she should just die. It's hard for me to even type those words right now, but I'm being completely transparent. We all read the news and hear what happens to some kids who are being relentlessly targeted. That very thing had happened in our neighborhood a few years earlier and was a constant reminder to me that so many kids are hurting much more than they let on.

As if all this weren't enough, Caroline began experiencing the same mean-girl dynamics on her club soccer team. The team had been a safe haven for her since junior high, but now the social equilibrium was shifting as the girls let their competitive natures take over. They started treating one another less as teammates and more as competition as they fought to attract the attention of college coaches who came to recruit them. I'd never felt more helpless than when I watched many of those friendships fall apart. As a mom, you can give all the pep talks you want about insecurity and jealousy and how it's just a season that will pass, but none of those talks really do much to ease the heart of a lonely teenage girl who just wants to have friends and feel there is a place she belongs.

It's upsetting to see your child hurt while you feel powerless to change anything. If you've walked with them through a really hard season, then I bet you know exactly what I'm talking about. Nothing prepares you for how painful it feels or the anxiety you constantly fight as you watch them struggle even when you trust that God is using the hard experiences to shape them into who He means for them to become.

Although Caroline blocked some of the girls so they couldn't keep contacting her, there wasn't a way to block what was happening in the halls at school or in the stands during Friday night football games. I thought of a million solutions—she could change schools, be homeschooled, move to a new city—but every time I prayed about it, I sensed God telling me to be still and trust Him. So I tried my best to do exactly that. Sometimes the way to get through something difficult is to keep your head up, fix your eyes on God, and walk through it even when you feel as though all you're doing is barely limping along. There are things He wants to forge in us that can be found only along the hardest paths we walk.

CHAPTER 15

Carrying Your Own Bucket

A couple of months ago, Caroline and I were having a conversation about the way she was raised. These are the kinds of things you can reflect on once your child is twenty and you have a pretty clear view of what worked and where you could have done better. Not that there's much you can do about it at that point. I guess it's more the opportunity to go on a parental apology tour where you can say, "Wow, we really got that wrong. Maybe we were too intense during some of your soccer games." And by "we," I mean Perry. I always acted perfectly normal and never one time wanted to fight a ref for making a bad call. It was more like four or five times.

Okay, six—tops.

As we talked, Caroline said, "Do you remember what Dad told me that one time at the ranch about carrying a bucket?"

I replied, "No. I don't remember a story about a bucket."

She went on, "Well, when I was about ten, I was at the ranch with Dad. We were walking around the fishing tank, and I was carrying a bucket that I'd been filling up with rocks and other stuff all day long. I tried to hand the bucket to Dad and asked if he'd carry it for me because it was getting heavy, and he told me, 'Nope, you have to carry your own bucket. When I was ten, my dad was dead and I didn't have a dad to carry my bucket. You have to carry your own bucket.'"

Listen, no one has ever accused Perry Shankle of attending the school of gentle parenting. Caroline and I both laughed until we cried as she recounted this bucket story, which I'd thankfully never heard until that very moment. But then she wiped her eyes as our laughter subsided and said, "You know what, though? That was harsh, but it was true. Dad has always taught me to do things for myself because you can't always depend on the people around you. It's served me well over the years. It gave me grit. He made me strong."

I'm grateful to Perry for so many things, but I think the way he has always known how to parent Caroline is at the top of the list. Those two are so similar in the way they perceive the world, which has allowed him to have insight into what she needs and how to help her. On the other hand, I know that my relationship with my mom caused me to overcompensate and go overboard in a well-intentioned attempt to prevent Caroline from feeling any pain or discomfort when she was growing up. That is great in theory, but pain and discomfort are also the building blocks that form character and resilience. They are a necessary part of growth for all of us and are often the very things God knows we need to fulfill who He is calling us to be. You can't raise a delicate flower in a greenhouse and then expect it to survive out in the wild without hardening it by exposing it to the elements. Perry and I have agreed that there were times he was too harsh and needed to be softer and times I coddled

Caroline too much and had to let go. It's all about finding the balance, which is often precarious. And there's nothing like parenting to really test what you know to be true versus what you wish were true.

I realized when she was very young that Caroline was not, in fact, my mini-me. She looked a lot like me. At times, she even acted like me. But she was very much her own person with her own view of the world. God also allowed me to have a clear sense of the gifts He'd given her. At an early age, she had discernment, insight into people's motives, and a bent toward leadership. I knew that my role as her mom was to encourage those gifts and help her develop them even though her perspective on things sometimes confounded me because it was so different from my own.

I knew now how important my mental and spiritual health was going to be over the ensuing years in order to parent Caroline in a way that would help her use all her gifts rather than my tamping them down to make myself feel more comfortable. I have always prayed that God would give me wisdom to know where her rough edges needed to be smoothed out and where they needed to remain. I wanted to love Caroline in a way that allowed her to be fully herself, because I'd been raised to feel as if I had to sacrifice parts of who I was to broker what was ultimately a false, fragile peace between my mom and me. I wanted more than that in my relationship with Caroline. I wanted her to always know that her whole self was fully seen and loved and also challenge her in areas where she needed to do better.

In the middle of all the heartache during her sophomore year, I had to travel for a speaking engagement. Isn't that one of the most difficult parts of walking through a really hard time with your child? The world doesn't stop as you mourn what is happening, and you have to proceed as if everything is okay and your heart isn't breaking into a million pieces.

As soon as I arrived at the hotel, I called home to check in with my people, and that's when I found out Caroline had another terrible day at school. I wished desperately that I weren't so far away. It's an awful feeling to know that your child is hurting and to not be able to be there to help. And that was really the breaking point. We were all just emotionally wrung out, and I couldn't remember the last time she'd had a good day at school. I was out of encouraging words about "turning the other cheek." I decided to call the mother of one of the girls who was sending cruel texts to ask if she knew what was going on. As we talked, she told me that she'd seen the texts but that it was just "girls being girls." I was stunned. Your child telling my child to "kill herself and make the world a better place" is just girls being girls? In what world? Some dystopian universe I don't know about?

I told this mother that the behavior and threats had to stop. I wasn't looking for the girls to be friends again; I was just asking that her child leave my child alone. All we wanted was peace. Her response was essentially that I was blowing things out of proportion and that none of it was that big of a deal. And in that moment, I had the clearest realization: Our kids become who we allow them to be. If we choose to ignore our child's bad behavior or justify it as kids being kids, we're condoning every bit of it. Mean mothers will raise mean girls if we don't stop the cycle.

Why aren't we teaching our girls to be better than this? Why aren't we showing them that there's enough out there for everyone and we don't need to feel insecure or see other women as our competition? Whatever we value or pay the most attention to in our children's lives are the things we're telling them are the most important. So if they see us focus on social standing, athletic achievements, academic prowess, and material things more than on kindness, contentment, humility, and respect, we're failing them as humans.

I would be lying if I told you I was functioning normally during these months. I looked normal on the outside, but I walked around like a ghost. I managed to buy groceries and cook dinner and cheer at soccer games. But I was broken inside. I had countless sleepless nights where I tossed and turned and prayed for God to give us a break. I was out of answers and desperately just wanted to do the right thing for my girl, but I had no idea what that even was at this point.

Every day seemed worse than the day before. Parenting a toddler is physically exhausting. Parenting a teen is maybe one of the most emotionally and mentally draining things a person can do. It's like just when you think you've reached an easier stage of parenting, you realize it's only fake spring. Trying to assess a situation and then counsel your child on how to deal with everything coming their way, while also trying to figure out whether they bear any responsibility for other kids' bad behavior, is a math problem that none of us will really ever be able to figure out. I was so tired and just so sad. It wasn't the way life was supposed to be.

We finally got to a point where enough was enough. The toxic dynamics had been going on for months and showed no signs of getting any better. We'd tried everything, and Caroline had been determined to handle the situation on her own without Perry and me intervening. We respected that for as long as we could. But after she had yet another rotten day at school, Perry told Caroline, "You've tried to be nice. You've tried to have the conversations. You've ignored them. You've done all the right things, but this is war, and it's time to fight back."

I immediately saw her countenance change. I'm a peacemaker at my core, well trained after a lifetime of trying to make everyone around me happy, so I'd been encouraging her to just be kind, not respond, try to ride it out, and take the high road. The problem was that none of those things were working. What she needed at that moment was to know it was okay to stand up for herself. If people are going to continue to come at you with venom, you don't have to stand there and take it. Perry told her, "If they follow you into the bathroom again, you tell them you are going straight to the high school administration. If they attempt physical violence, you punch them in the face. We will meet you in the office. This is over."

At that moment, her dad carried her bucket as he spoke the words she needed to hear. Perry set her free to be herself. She was tired of being passive. I'd been trying to get her to handle it the way I would, but then God showed me that He'd equipped her to get through it in her own way with the strength, resilience, and grit He'd given her. She was a warrior who needed to fight back. What I realized was that the battle wasn't between Caroline and those girls; it was about her finding real peace with who she was and what she knew to be right. I felt relieved by this revelation but also scared of what it might look like for her to walk it out.

The next day, the girls confronted her in the bathroom, where all teenage cowards from the dawn of time have chosen to stalk their prey, and she didn't back down. She told them exactly what she was going to do, and she did it. The administration stepped in and implemented disciplinary steps that ensured that either the harassment would stop or the girls would face more severe consequences.

Should we have stepped in earlier? I don't know. It's so hard to figure out how long to let your child fight their own battles. But God gave us the wisdom to know that it was definitely time to step in and give Caroline what she needed to advocate for herself. Here's the hard part: That timing is going to look different for every child.

I wish I could write this book as though it's a ten-step program, with simple answers on how to get through the treacherous waters of dealing with mean girls. But while so many factors are the same, others will vary depending on the personalities involved and the way God has equipped your child. Maybe what worked for us isn't the right solution for you. But Caroline is a fighter. It's who she is. She needed to know that it was okay to stand up for herself. It took her some time to get there, but once she was done, she was done. That isn't going to be the way every girl handles it.

When I look back at the years I spent contorting myself into some modified version of who I really was in failed attempts to make my mom happy, I realize I desire peace at any cost. For years, I blamed myself for things that weren't my fault. Self-blame is going to be the default for so many of us as people gaslight us or even as we gaslight ourselves into believing things might be better if we could just be different.

I believe the key is to recognize your child's strengths and weaknesses and then guide them in the way that fits who they truly are, not who you want them to be. And the only way to really do that is to ask God for the wisdom to see (and the courage to be) who you need to be for them to become who they are meant to be. That isn't easy, and it doesn't come without some pain. But I do believe it's part of what Proverbs 27:17 tells us: "As iron sharpens iron, so one person sharpens another." I can tell you from the number of times Perry has decided to sharpen knives in our kitchen while I'm trying to relax that it isn't a quiet, delicate process. It's grating and jarring and sometimes causes sparks to fly.

Throughout that dreadful sophomore year, Perry and I stuck closer to Caroline than ever before. Teens want to act as if they don't really need or want you around at this time, when in fact they desperately need you. When their whole world is shaking around them, your home needs to be a safe space, a harbor from the storm, a place where they know they are unconditionally loved. And, man, there is such power in our prayers when we ask God to let our kids see themselves through His eyes and hinder every arrow the Enemy throws at them so that instead of destroying our teens, any trauma would instead raise up warriors equipped to fight the battles we all ultimately face.

God used in this experience so much of what I'd encountered growing up with a toxic mother. I was able to fully recognize the behavior of these girls toward Caroline for what it was, and I used that knowledge to try to help her realize that none of it was really about her or anything she'd done.

For years, I watched my mom operate out of her insecurities and jealousy. She threw away perfectly good relationships because of her failure to get out of her own way, and she lashed out at people for no real reason other than her own inability to find lasting peace and joy. Caroline and I had so many conversations about the way broken people operate and the tendencies they have to tear down another person to make themselves feel better. I recognized how these girls went after Caroline's physical appearance, targeted the places where she already felt insecure, twisted her words, and resented every bit of happiness she found. I saw the way she felt like she couldn't let her guard down because they were constantly looking for a fight.

The patterns were so familiar to me that I realized God had uniquely enabled me to help Caroline deal with them. However, being able to do that in a healthy way meant I had to be healed and whole to help her navigate the situation. I saw the ways God had gone before me all those years earlier and given me the strength to sever the relationship with my mom. He knew what I was going to need in order to become strong long before I did. Without my own emotional healing, I think I might have jumped on the mean-girl roller coaster and encouraged Caroline to go scorched earth. But from a healthy place, I was able to explain to her that mean girls are mean girls, whether they are in your family or in your classroom. And when you realize they aren't going to change, you have the freedom to walk away.

When you are in the midst of a fight with a dragon, it's hard to clearly see all the ways it's trying to attack. But after you've fought that enemy, you have better vision to see all the strategies it uses against you and how to defend yourself. It's not about fighting fire with fire; it's about fighting fire with the truth of the situation and recognizing all the dynamics at play. I did my best to teach Caroline that there are always going to be dragons in our paths looking to destroy us but that we aren't powerless once we realize the ways God has equipped us to fight them with His truth.

Now let me tell you the rest of the story. Sophomore year, as horrible as it was, generated a resilience and strength in Caroline that God knew she would need because she had a decision to make. Was she going to let these things break her, or was she going to use them to become stronger? With classic twenty-twenty hindsight, I can see the situation now in a way that I couldn't when it all just felt bleak and dismal and like it was about to destroy our daughter. We'd always told her that good things come from adversity, but that was the first time it had really been put to the test in her life. That was when the toddler who used to spit on the floor used that strong will for good. She adapted, refused to be a victim, and made the best of a really challenging situation by trusting God and holding on to her faith. It gave her resolve to overcome the toughest parts of her story. She worked hard to become captain of the soccer team, graduate with honors, and get accepted to Texas A&M—her dream school. But those were all things we couldn't see at the time. We had to walk blindly along a path that was so painful, trusting God to show us the way.

Your child will undoubtedly face their own dragons. It's going to look different for you, depending on the situation and their personality and temperament. I encourage you to figure out what they need. Maybe it will be to change schools or get counseling. The timeline for results isn't predictable either. Some kids will continue to struggle until they eventually find themselves in a new season of life and in a bigger pond than your typical junior high or high school. (More on that in chapter 17.) There's no blanket right answer to dealing with a situation; there's just the right answer for your child. As a parent, your job is to really see their strengths and their weaknesses so you can guide them and protect them as they fight the battles that will shape who they are.

In our story, all the prayers I'd prayed for Caroline to be a strong, resilient leader were at least partly answered during her sophomore year as she developed character and empathy and realized the importance of being true to your faith and your values even when no one is looking. She grew so much that year and understood that there was no reason to diminish the strong, unique personality God has given her; He made her that way for a reason. It's an important lesson for me to remember now, years later, as she faces other hard circumstances. It's all these tough, character-building parts of life that can foster strength in us in fundamental ways. It may sound cliché, but so often the only way to fight a battle effectively is to go through it, not around it.

I'd prayed from the earliest days of being Caroline's mom that God would use the unique qualities He'd given her to make her bold and brave—a leader who would point the people around her to Him. I wanted her to be a strong warrior in a world I knew was going to present a lot of battles. But I was too naïve to realize when I prayed that prayer that none of those things would just happen without her character being built through circumstances that have often been difficult. In his book *Those Who Remain*, G. Michael Hopf said, "Hard times create strong men, strong men create good times, good times create weak men, and weak men create hard times."[1] We live in a time in history when we need strong men and women perhaps more than ever before. And how do we create that if we try to constantly protect them from the very things God is using to sharpen them and make them effective leaders?

Of course, this is easier said than done. It takes strength and reliance on God to show us how to parent in healthy ways. Our trust in God, not pat answers or clever parenting techniques, will make the biggest difference in our lives and in the lives of our children.

CHAPTER 16

Stopping the Mean-Girl Cycle

Several years ago, Perry was talking to a guy who's a wildlife expert and asked him what was one of the meanest animals he's ever encountered. He replied, "Pound for pound? Not much that's more ferocious than a North American river otter." Who knew that otters were mean? Not me. And I would contend that, pound for pound, many teenage girls could give a river otter a run for its money. I bet most of us can think back on a situation where we were the target of a mean girl who wanted to tear us down. It's an epidemic.

I wish, dear reader, that I could encourage you at this juncture and tell you that the rest of Caroline's high school years were wonderful and filled with magic and that they ended with a fun carnival where everyone danced and sang like in the movie *Grease*. But that would be a lie. Add in a worldwide pandemic that began at the end of her junior year, along with an almost career-ending soccer injury, and what you have is the complete antithesis of an ideal experience. It was all an uphill battle that felt like it would never end. The physical injuries she endured from soccer, the protocols we all had to follow because of Covid-19, and a homecoming and senior prom that were canceled were external signs of all the things I was mourning internally as I watched our daughter struggle every step of the way. Things were never as hard again as they were during her sophomore year, but she never really found her people. Instead of dreading the day that she'd graduate from high school and head to college, I began to count down the days. It felt like she just needed a fresh start in a new place. Perry and I continued to point her to God and the fact that only He could fill all those lonely places in her heart. We encouraged her to look to Him for her security and her identity. I told her that college would be the place where she would find her people. I said it so much that I got scared I was overselling it. And none of those things really help ease the heart of a girl who's hurting, lonely, and tired of spending weekends hanging out with her parents.

It has taken getting on the other side of Caroline's high school experience and thinking back on what she went through with mean girls for me to really be able to process and reflect on what creates this culture. A big part of the problem is that we don't even realize how often we are pushing our kids to be a better version of *our*selves—or are attempting to live vicariously through them in the hope they achieve things we never did—as opposed to being the best version of who God made *them* to be. This creates a disconnect in their souls, especially when we focus on their accolades and accomplishments rather than who they are. The world tells us success looks like athletic prowess, academic achievement, social standing, and physical perfection, while God tells us it looks like loving our neighbor, lifting others up, controlling our emotions, and having a humble spirit.

Watching our daughters struggle is just the hardest, partly because doing so tends to reopen our own old wounds that we thought were completely healed, only to find out that there are places where we are still tender from past damage. After I wrote *Nobody's Cuter than You,* I spent months doing interviews and talking about female friendship. Every time, at least one woman would come up to me to talk about how hurt she'd been by the actions of another woman she'd thought was a friend. As I've traveled around the country and occasionally talked about Caroline's high school experience, the topic of mean friends is always what resonates most. Women approach me afterward to share about a time they went through friendship trials or tell me they have a daughter who is currently going through something similar. We all feel so helpless. This is the ever-present pandemic that no one knows how to stop.

In the fall of 2021, the CDC conducted a survey that revealed what I believe we already knew: Teen girls are in crisis. The report stated, "Nearly 1 in 3 (30%) seriously considered attempting suicide—up nearly 60% from a decade ago." It also said that "nearly 3 in 5 (57%) U.S. teen girls felt persistently sad or hopeless in 2021—double that of boys."[1]

We are living in the fallout of a culture where social media is prevalent and makes teen girls feel as if everyone else is better, smarter, and prettier. We are a society that makes people famous for no real reason at all, puts people on pedestals, and then just as quickly decides to tear them down. We bought into the lie that we need to focus on building up self-esteem in girls, which causes them to focus inward, as opposed to self-respect, which shows them that the way to find joy and contentment is to believe in something bigger than themselves. The secret to curbing mean-girl behavior is to raise a girl to know that no other woman's success undermines what God wants to do in her own life.

If there's one thing my life's experience has taught me, it's that we have to allow God to heal what has been broken in us if we are going to have any chance of raising our daughters in a healthy manner. And in order to heal our brokenness, we first have to recognize it. As I alluded to earlier, I didn't recognize all the mean-girl behavior my mom exhibited toward me through-out my life until I watched Caroline begin to deal with those same things during her sophomore year. Maybe for you it was a different relative, a friend, or a schoolmate who belittled you or constantly made you feel less than.

Mean girls are all just slight variations of a standard package: They gaslight you into believing things are your fault, they pick apart your physical appearance, they let you know all the ways you aren't good enough, and they are consistently passive-aggressive. Any interaction with them makes you feel like you're walking on eggshells so as not to anger them, and they resent any success or happiness you might find. They look for ways to make you feel bad about yourself, and they make you feel para-noid that people are always saying bad things about you, be-cause, well, *they* are always saying bad things about you behind your back. They will take the very things you consider to be strengths of your personality and turn them into negatives: "You're too loud." "You try too hard." "You take up too much space in a room." They will make threats to harm themselves and tell you it'll be your fault if they do. They can be vicious and verbally abusive but then cunning enough to turn it around and make it seem like you deserved it. In summary, they create an emotionally toxic atmosphere for the people in their paths.

When I had to witness this playing out in Caroline's life, I had to take a deep breath and say a lot of prayers to remind myself that I was the adult in the situation. I had the experience of dealing with so much of that behavior at the hands of my mom and other mean girls I encountered along the way, but I couldn't allow myself to jump into the fray with Caroline and fight back with the same toxic behavior. Doing so might have felt good in the moment and created a sort of unhealthy bond as we fought a common enemy, but that wouldn't have been the sound way to handle it. Part of the solution is to recognize that the people who have hurt us are operating out of their own wounds that they've never allowed to heal. We've got to stop the vicious loop of toxic behavior, and that means taking the higher road even when it's the harder road.

Spoiler alert: It's always the harder road. But it's also a road that gives you the freedom to stand up for yourself and walk away. And that is my best advice if you're currently dealing with toxic people in your life. You can wish them well, shake the dust from your feet, and walk away.

I don't have the answers for how to stop all the terrible dynamics that occur with regularity among teenage girls—girls who are rooted in insecurity and lack a spiritual compass. And although we can't control how other girls are being raised, we can control how we are raising our own daughters. One of the values we need to pass down is the beauty of female friendship and what it adds to our lives. We need to let our girls know that there is room for everyone and show them what it looks like to cheer on the women around us. We need to quit our tendency to substitute the joy of real relationships with cheap imitations like Snapchat and Instagram that only serve to make all of us feel more insecure. We need to quit measuring our lives against someone else's, because, from the outside looking in, we never really know what another person is going through. And ultimately, we need to find our worth in trusting that God has unique plans for our lives that will look different from what He has for those around us.

A few weeks ago, I had a conversation with a woman whose daughter is two years younger than Caroline and having a hard time with friend dynamics. I shared with the woman that we'd dealt with many of those same things. Wide-eyed, she looked at me and exclaimed, "Really? I had no idea! It always seemed like Caroline was having an incredible high school experience!" I've thought back on that often because it reminds me that we never know the path someone else is having to walk. This was true of my own childhood, where no one realized that I was constantly belittled at home, and it was true of Caroline's high school years. It's also true of people we interact with online. We've all learned to perfectly curate our social media posts to show the high points rather than the loneliness and heartache we may be experiencing at any given time.

Although I don't have all the answers to mean-girl problems, God does. His Word is full of instruction we can apply. Let's look at a few examples.

GOD TELLS US HOW TO TREAT ONE ANOTHER

As God's chosen people, holy and dearly loved, clothe your-selves with compassion, kindness, humility, gentleness and patience. Bear with each other and forgive one another if any of you has a grievance against someone. Forgive as the Lord forgave you. And over all these virtues put on love, which binds them all together in perfect unity. (Colossians 3:12–14)

How different would we be if we all did our best to live that out daily? I believe we need to encourage our kids to reach out to those who are hurting or alone. As I said earlier, it's so easy to just go with the flow until your child is the one on the receiving end of mean-girl behavior. I had a mom tell me a couple of years ago after her daughter was abandoned by a group of girlfriends, "Not one of those mothers reached out to me or bothered to ask their daughter, 'Hey, what happened with Katie?' It's like we ceased to exist." Let's teach our girls by example that we need to look out for one another and be friends to those in need. There are fault lines just below the surface in so many people's lives we won't even see unless there's an earthquake.

GOD TELLS US WHO WE REALLY ARE

We are God's handiwork, created in Christ Jesus to do good works, which God prepared in advance for us to do. (Ephesians 2:10)

Let's show our kids where their true identity and security are found. Each of us is wonderfully and fearfully made, and God has put us in our families, schools, communities, and world in this time for very specific and unique reasons. Instead of making ourselves feel better by making someone else feel small and insignificant, we can feel empowered and confident as we run our own race to discover the purposes for which God has created us. That's the point of the race.

GOD TELLS US HOW TO RAISE OUR KIDS

Train up a child in the way he should go;
    even when he is old he will not depart from it. (Proverbs 22:6, esv)

The thing is—and I know this from how often I want to skip my workouts—training isn't that easy or fun most of the time. I would like to lift weights once every six months and have arms that look great in sleeveless tops, but I regret to tell you that it doesn't work that way. Raising kids to be kind also takes perseverance and consistency. It takes sacrifice and commitment as we spend eighteen short—let's be honest: *lightning-fast*—years pouring into them and equipping them to be responsible, productive, and, ideally, employed adults.

GOD TELLS US HOW TO ACT

What does the Lord require of you?
To act justly and to love mercy
    and to walk humbly with your God. (Micah 6:8)

Our kids will model what they see from us far more than listen to what we say. If the way we treat others and see our own peers doesn't line up with what we say, then it's all a fruitless exercise.

GOD TELLS US THE CHARACTERISTICS WE NEED

The fruit of the Spirit is love, joy, peace, forbearance, kindness, goodness, faithfulness, gentleness and self-control. Against such things there is no law. Those who belong to Christ Jesus have crucified the flesh with its passions and desires. Since we live by the Spirit, let us keep in step with the Spirit. Let us not become conceited, provoking and envying each other. (Galatians 5:22–26)

Parents who show their kids how to walk in the Spirit will raise children who follow in their footsteps. Will we raise perfect children? One hundred percent no. Are there going to be times when we see them get caught up in ugly behavior and we worry that we're failing? Yep. Welcome to parenting. It's the most humbling experience of your life.

However, we have the privilege of being the loudest voice our children hear during their most critical years. This means we have the responsibility to break any of our own unhealthy patterns and ask God to help us do a new thing in the lives of our children that will be a gift to the world around them. We have to be obedient to cut off what is sick or dead in our own lives so that we can show our kids what it looks like to bear fruit.

I know that the darkness wants to come for our kids, and the most effective way for the Enemy to do that in the lives of young people, who are designed to crave connection, is to use those very relationships to tear them down. Voices are everywhere, whispering to them that they're less than, that they're inadequate, that they'll never be enough, and that their lives don't matter. Bullying has gone on from the beginning of time and has never been easier now that we can hide behind a keyboard while giving voice to the worst of our humanity. But I also know that our kids are looking to us to model appropriate behavior. They may not act like it or acknowledge it, but they know better than anyone if the person we appear to be outside our home is the same person we are inside.

So let's ask God for the strength to be principled people, the wisdom to know how to raise principled people, and the grace to forgive one another when we fall short. In the words of my pastor, Sean Azzaro, "We can't parent perfectly, but we can parent faithfully." That involves leading by example.

CHAPTER 17

Go Make Something
of Yourself, Kid

As I write this chapter, Perry and I have officially been empty nesters for almost two and a half years, although we prefer the term coined by my friend Patti: *free birds*. It just sounds so much better and doesn't conjure up depressing connotations of being barren and lifeless. People don't talk much about this stage of life, and when they do, it's usually with dread and sadness. Women seem to dream about the day they'll get married or have kids or what kind of mom they'll be, but no one really says, "Man, you know what'll be awesome? When all my kids move out of the house and leave me all by myself with no real sense of purpose." I mean, when you really think about it, it's kind of bizarre that we raise these kids for eighteen years and pour our hearts and souls and checkbooks into them and then one day they just say, "Thanks for the food and lodging and unconditional love, but I'm going to go live in a dirty frat house now."

What I didn't know about these years was how much joy and contentment can be found when you get here. Don't get me wrong: It definitely takes some time to adjust to a new kind of normal. But there is sweetness on the other side of all the soccer car pools, last-minute science projects, and packed lunches that no one eats and that only serve to test the expiration limits of a bunch of grapes. I also didn't know how much time Perry and I would spend discussing what we think our dogs are probably saying to us. And I regret to tell you that we've become a Progressive commercial, as evidenced by Perry picking up the phone while I was cooking dinner the other night to call our neighbor Tom to let him know that a branch on his pecan tree was hanging at a precarious angle. I'd like to say I'm better than that, but I just ordered Halloween costumes for our dogs, so who am I to judge anyone? What you don't know when people are telling you to invest in your 401(k) for retirement is that you're going to need that money because you become a person who will purchase dog costumes with hard-earned American dollars purely for amusement.

But let me back up and tell you about the end of Caroline's high school years and the process of launching her out into the world, because it is a whole thing for a mom's heart. Because of the pandemic, Caroline's senior year was a bizarre mix of emotions. I was thankful for every milestone that wasn't canceled, but there were also so many days she was just doing online school at home because of quarantine protocols. It made me increasingly aware of how much she needed to expand her horizons and get out of this space she'd clearly outgrown. The pandemic only heightened the isolation and loneliness that had defined so much of her last three years. But that didn't mean I didn't have a knot in my stomach at every "last" moment of the high school experience.

The night she played her last varsity soccer game, I could barely make it to the car before breaking down in tears. Soccer had been such a huge part of our lives from the time she was six years old. We've already discussed how I initially enrolled her in ballet class at age three but she mistakenly assumed it was a competitive sport—against the girls in her own performance. That led us to soccer, and we spent the next twelve years watching her play on fields all over the country. We cheered her on as she ran on the field every week, washed more soccer jerseys than I care to remember, pulled cleats that smelled like the devil's footwear out of backpacks, iced injuries, made midnight trips to the orthopedic ER, gave infinite pep talks, and yelled at refs. We had the thrill of watching her score game-winning goals and the devastation of watching her carted off the field with injuries. But it developed her character—her strong will and tenacity. It taught her what leadership really looks like on and off the field. It made her better, stronger, and more resilient than she would have been without it and gave us some of our favorite memories as a family. And now it was all over. I trusted that God would lead her to new fields and different adventures, but I still cried for about two weeks as I grieved the end of this era.

A few weeks later, just days before graduation, I saw a huge shift in her. I can only describe it as watching someone about to complete a grueling marathon gain a burst of energy as they realize they are almost to the finish line. There was a light in her eyes that hadn't been there in a long time and just a complete freedom to be every bit of herself. A new kind of boldness and fearlessness began to emerge in her as she saw the horizon of a new life ahead. It was as if her high school years had been a walk through a carnival fun house with mirrors that tried to distort her vision of herself, obstacles that popped out of nowhere to test her resolve, and trials that threw her off-balance and made her question what she believed.

But I saw this relief in her as she began to realize that she'd navigated the maze, fought the dragons, and made it through to the exit door. She'd made sacrifices and tough decisions. She'd learned that often the right way is the path that leaves you feeling lonely. And trying to hold her back now would be as fruitless as trying to hold back the wind. She was ready to fly.

Perry and I had watched her grow from a funny, headstrong little girl into a confident, poised woman who knows who she is and what she wants out of life. And although I still felt sad that her growing-up years were behind us, I was so excited for what was ahead, because I saw a girl ready to set the world on fire. What my young mom self who rocked her baby to sleep seventeen years earlier didn't know, as she dreaded the day that baby would graduate from high school, was how God was going to prepare and equip all of us for what was next.

I spent the summer after Caroline's graduation channeling all my complex emotions into buying things off Amazon for her dorm room, and she used that time to cut essentially all remaining ties to her high school life. What I remember most about that summer is that she spent her days working at a veterinary clinic and her nights just hanging out on the couch with Perry and me. While we loved having all this time with her, I also knew that it wasn't the way it was supposed to be and prayed for her to have loyal, true friends in her life.

I began to count down the days until she would leave for college and her world would finally open up to a bigger space where she would hopefully find her people. We watched a lot of old movies that summer, classics we felt she needed to see before we sent her out into the world. This included *The Electric Horseman*. At the end of the movie (spoiler alert—but since it came out in 1979, you've had time to see it), Robert Redford sets Rising Star free to run with all the wild horses. As Redford takes off the horse's bridle to let him loose, he charges him with "Make something out of yourself now."[1]

That scene was all I could think about as we moved Caroline into the dorm that August and prepared to say our goodbyes. It was her time to run free and be everything she was meant to be. I've never experienced so many emotions at once, but there was much peace and joy to be found knowing that she was moving into a place that was exactly where God wanted her and that He had her in His hands. It was her time to make something out of herself, and we couldn't wait to watch her run free, even though our hearts ached as we watched her walk away.

During her first year of college, God was so faithful to redeem what Caroline lost in high school. It all began when she went to Impact, a Christian orientation camp for freshmen at Texas A&M. I picked her up after her three days at camp and could see a difference in her. On the ride home, she told me that she hadn't really believed there were kids her age who took their faith seriously but that Impact had shown her that wasn't true. Over the next year, God surrounded her with amazing friends, great experiences, and more fun than she could usually pack into her days (based on how little sleep she got). She came home one weekend in late September and announced she was so proud of herself for "stopping at Buc-ee's and getting gas and a blue raspberry Icee like a real grown-up."

We could tell she was exhausted, though, so Perry and I gave her a long lecture about how she had to prioritize sleep or she would get sick. Before she drove back to school that Sunday, she promised us she would do better, so I was surprised at what she said when she called me at eight o'clock that Monday morning. I answered the phone and asked, "Why are you awake this early?" because I knew she didn't have an early-morning class.

She replied, "Well, actually I never went to bed because a whole group of us camped out all night for football tickets."

What I'm saying is she clearly was taking all her parents' advice to heart. Or not.

A few weeks after that, I drove to College Station to have lunch with her. She had a terrible cough, and in this time period so soon after Covid-19, I told her, "You can't walk around coughing like that. You're going to become a pariah." I drove her to the clinic to get it checked out.

While we were there, she got a notification that her first college quiz score had been posted. She'd made a fifty. She burst into tears as she confessed that she was having a great time but was also homesick and school was hard and dorm bathrooms were gross and how was she going to recover from a fifty on a quiz? I tried to encourage her as we drove through the line at Chick-fil-A to get her an eight-count nugget meal before I dropped her back off at the dorm with her hacking cough and antibiotics.

We sat in the parking lot for a while, and I told her, "This is all part of the process. College is hard, and you have to adjust to a new normal. But look at all the good things going on in your life. Look at the friends you've made and the fun you're having."

She tearfully agreed as she blew her nose multiple times and hugged me really tight before she got out of the car and walked up to her dorm room. I sat there for a few more minutes, reflecting on everything we'd just talked about and hoping she would be okay. Then I looked at my passenger seat—which was now covered in chicken-nugget crumbs, snotty napkins, and a half-eaten container of waffle fries—and thought, *Whoever thinks motherhood ends when you drop them off at college is completely mistaken. That's fake summer.*

Here's a truth that you already know if you're in this stage: Mothering your child goes on to some degree for the rest of your life. The whole empty-nest thing is kind of a lie. Your house might be empty, your pantry is definitely barer, but your mind is as full as it has ever been with thoughts of your child. You never quit worrying, guiding, coaching, and cheering them on. There are endless pep talks and prayers. It's an infinite stretch of hoping, advising, and loving. And you'll never convince me that it's not the hardest, best job in the whole world. As I sat in my car and caught my breath after all the emotions I'd had and the cheerleading I'd done, I was just so thankful that God had given me the strength to change the narrative of the first half of my life with my own mother, and the wisdom and fortitude to become the mother I wished I'd had by breaking a destructive cycle.

And I was also thankful for a husband who notices if a neighbor's tree limb is hanging in a precarious position.

CHAPTER 18

Waiting for the Blooms

Sometime during the spring of Caroline's freshman year of college, I was out walking the dogs. It was a glorious day in Texas. (We have to enjoy those before summer comes and tries to kill us.) Walking with the dogs is when I do some of my best thinking and praying since there are no distractions, except when Mabel decides to act like an idiot, such as when she thinks it's a good idea to try to take on a cat.

As I walked, I noticed that all the mountain laurel trees in the neighborhood were blooming. I don't know if you know about mountain laurels, but they have the most beautiful purple blossoms and make the air smell like grape soda. They are my favorite part of spring in San Antonio. We had one in our yard that hadn't flowered in years, despite Perry trying everything he knew to do to get it to bloom. He'd cut off dead branches, pruned it at all the right times, fertilized it, and made sure the roots were getting enough light. Yet it still wouldn't bloom. I don't know why, because I'm not a botanist. I just know that it had been a real disappointment. Year after year, I wondered why all the other trees in the neighborhood were doing so well when my tree just looked bleak.

That day with Piper and Mabel, though, as I rounded the corner toward our house, I looked up and realized our tree was covered in blossoms for the first time in years. And I know enough about horticulture to know it didn't just happen. That tree had been working to produce flowers long before it did. I just couldn't see that part. All I saw was nothing happening, but clearly it had needed time to be healthy enough to bloom. Meanwhile, it was a tree that looked sad and empty. And isn't that just how God works? There are times when everything can seem barren. There are seasons of life that are excruciatingly hard and filled with so much pain and emptiness. We have to cut away the parts that are dead even though it feels like it may take us down. Our tree looks desolate while everyone else's trees seem to be blooming in abundance.

But what God showed me through our mountain laurel that day was that He is always working, even when we don't see it. Where we look and see nothing, He looks and sees the whole picture of the way our lives will eventually bear fruit if we just hold on and trust Him. He is already answering those prayers you are praying, but sometimes you can't see that until the tree in your yard bursts into bloom. Then you realize He was always at work.

Over the course of Caroline's past two years of college, I've watched her grow in ways I never could have envisioned. I've witnessed her having incredible relationships and experiences I never imagined. I thought back to the end of her freshman year, when she applied to be a counselor at Impact—the camp that had such a huge influence on her. She had me proofread her application. When I got to the part where she'd written her testimony, I was undone.

The summer before college, I felt something stirring in me. I knew I had to be strong for a little bit longer. I cut off everyone from high school that was dragging me down. I was without friends, and it was an extremely hard time. I went to Impact, and my world exploded. God's goodness overwhelmed me, and for the first time, I felt hope, light, and love in my life. I realized what it truly felt like to be saved by Christ. God lit a fire in my soul, and I knew my life was about to make a total one-eighty. My heart softened. I let people in and found community. I realized that nothing in the world could ever be better than Jesus, and my life has looked different ever since. This past semester has been the best thing in my whole life. Every day, God heals more of me and teaches me something new.

Knowing what I know now (but couldn't see at the time), would I go back and change one thing about her high school experience if I could?

Not in a million years.

As we moved Caroline out of the dorm at the end of her freshman year, I kept thinking that it felt like we'd just moved her in a week ago. We looked around the empty dorm room, and she said, "This has been the best year of my life."

And because moms know these things, I can attest it really had been. What college has given my girl over the past couple of years has been beyond anything I prayed for. The way she has grown in her faith, the incredible friends she has made, the professors and advisers who have guided her, the Aggies beating Alabama at Kyle Field—it's all been Ephesians 3:20 in action.

When she left home after high school, it felt like an ending. But it has truly been the most beautiful beginning to the future God has written for her. It's given us a clearer vision of how He used her past struggles to uniquely equip her to step into what He had ahead. It's helped me see that sometimes the best prayer we can pray as parents is "God, this one is Yours. You are the author of her story, and I trust You to write an amazing one."

For a long time, her tree seemed so empty compared with everyone else's. But it was only because things were happening beyond what I could see—things that were about to produce more than I could have ever hoped for. And it made me realize that everything healthy that was developing in her life was a result of God giving Perry and me the wisdom and strength to break destructive patterns in our family line that limited our vision of how He saw us and what He could do if we were fully surrendered to Him.

Psalm 128:1–4 says,

Blessed are all who fear the Lord,
    who walk in obedience to him.
You will eat the fruit of your labor;
    blessings and prosperity will be yours.
Your wife will be like a fruitful vine
    within your house;
your children will be like olive shoots
    around your table.
Yes, this will be the blessing
    for the man who fears the Lord.

This means that when we, as parents, walk in obedience to what God is calling us to do, our children will flourish. The thing about olive shoots is they grow from the base of older, healthy trees and become so strong that they end up bearing fruit long after the older tree dies. The passage also says that the olive shoots are around your table, and I'm choosing to believe that means my child will want to spend most holidays with us.

It's a reminder to me—and I hope an encouragement to you—to keep the faith even when all seems lost or different than we expected. We can grieve for what we think we wanted life to look like, but there comes a time to pick ourselves up and live the life we've been given. Our trust in God's plans for our kids can't be dependent on everything always turning out like we hoped. Whatever life looks like for you is no less meaningful just because it looks different than you imagined.

And I want to say here that I also believe being a parent comes with no guarantees. We can do all the right things and pray all the right prayers, and our kids are still going to have struggles. God has given them the same free will that we all have, and sometimes they are going to make bad decisions no matter how hard we worked to prevent that.

One thing God has put on my heart during this season is that if I'm always trying to be Caroline's savior, then I'm not letting her lean into the fact that He is her Savior. The other night, Perry and I were talking during dinner about Caroline and a situation she is currently trying to work through. I said, "This stage is hard because she's really an adult and has to figure this out for herself."

Perry looked at me and replied, "Yeah, it's kind of like we can be offensive and defensive coordinators to some extent but we aren't in the game. But you know what? I trust my player. And more than that, I trust our Head Coach."

I appreciate nothing more than some wisdom wrapped in a sports analogy.

God may delay an answer to prayer, and hard times are inevitably going to happen, but He is always at work in ways we can't see. In the words of 1 Corinthians 2:9,

"What no eye has seen,
    what no ear has heard,
and what no human mind has conceived"—
    the things God has prepared for those who love him.

Eventually, the blooms will show up when you least expect it.

CHAPTER 19

Bulls and Blood, the Dust and Mud

There is something about being in my fifties and on the other side of a lot of life that has made me reflect back. So much of life, during the actual time it's happening, can be hard to process. It's only later that you can really see the handprint of God. I don't even think I realized until I was writing this book all the ways God has filled in the gap that my relationship with my mom left. For one, He gave me my dad and Cherrie, who have always loved and supported me and understood the difficulties in dealing with my mom and how that has affected me.

God also gave me my dear friend Gulley. When I arrived at Texas A&M as a student way back in 1989, God led me to Gulley, who had also grown up with a toxic parental relationship. And through Gulley, He gave me her mom, Honey, and her stepdad, Big, who have loved me like I was their own since I walked into their house. I always say that, at nineteen years old, I had no idea all the ways my own family was going to fall apart. But God did, and He surrounded me with people who have softened my landing.

Let's not overlook the gift of being married to a man like Perry, who really sees me and knows me. His encouragement and challenges have shaped me in ways that nothing else possibly could have. He is the steady home I spent so many years searching for.

And I'm also kind of astounded by all the close friends I have who know what it's like to live with a difficult parent. Either more of us are out there than I even realize, or God has just filled my life with people who really get what that looks like. Maybe there is some kind of force field that attracts us to one another. It's been such a comfort to me because I feel like we are all quick to assume that everyone has a normal, loving family except for us. If you tell someone who hasn't been in that position that you have cut your mother out of your life, it feels like there can be a lot of judgment. And each of my friends with a truly dysfunctional, unhealthy parent has chosen a different way to deal with it. There is no one right answer, which is why I would encourage anyone to really seek God's guidance and wisdom for how to handle your unique situation.

As I watched many of my friends deal with the death of a toxic parent, I wondered how I would feel when my mom died. Over the years, as I continued to be estranged from her, I continually prayed that God would give me discernment about repairing my relationship with her. I would occasionally do an emotional inventory of myself to see if I had any lingering bitterness or resentment toward her. It was like touching an old bruise to see if it had healed. And I knew more and more that the answer was no. I was no longer holding her prisoner for the things she couldn't be. Sometimes all you can do is come to terms with the truth of who people are, accept that you can't change them, and then move on.

· · · · · ·

I've heard people say that every generation blames the one before for the trials and struggles in their lives that seem to be directly correlated to the way they were raised. And as I look at my mom's life, I do wonder how many of her issues were due to having an overbearing mother who was always bent on controlling every possible narrative where her daughters were concerned. Nanny was a loving, doting grandmother to her grandkids, likely only because she'd softened considerably with age. But the hold she had on my mom was powerful. Truly, I think her relationship with her mother was the great love of Suzanne's life. There was a big part of Suzanne that would've been happy in a world that forever let her remain a child in her mom's house with no real responsibilities or decisions to make.

So it didn't surprise me that when Nanny's health continued to decline, my mom decided to move my grandma to Oklahoma to live at her house. Being a caretaker wasn't really in my mom's wheelhouse, but if there were ever going to be an exception to that rule, it was going to be for Nanny.

A few months after the move, Amy called to say that Nanny had passed away and that Mom was trying to figure out the best way to get Nanny from Oklahoma back to Texas. She'd wanted to be buried next to Big Bob in the small cemetery in Colmesneil, Texas, right around the corner from the lake house where our family had spent so much time. I didn't think much of this until she said, "Apparently, she can have Nanny flown back to Texas, but it's going to cost around five hundred dollars, and she doesn't want to spend that money. So she's decided she and James will just rent a van and drive her to the funeral home in Woodville." Although Amy had been giving me occasional reports on Mom's increasingly bizarre behavior over the years, nothing prepared me for this.

Whatever you might possibly be wondering about this scenario is something I was considering now: *Is that legal? Do the auto-rental people know what they're using the van for? Is this like a* Weekend at Bernie's *situation, or is she in a casket? Do you leave the van running when you stop to go to the bathroom or for lunch on the eight-hour drive? What is the etiquette on eating road-trip snacks like beef jerky and Sour Patch Kids when your deceased mother is riding in the back of a van?* It just felt like if there were ever a time to spend the money on a plane ticket, this was the time.

But that was a classic example of my mom getting an idea in her head and deciding the strangest option was the best option. Mom was determined to make a road trip to Texas with her dead mother even though she most assuredly could have afforded the plane ticket. Mom also took her dog with her on this ill-conceived trip. So the merry band of travelers consisted of James driving, my mom riding shotgun with her miniature poodle, Princess, in her lap, and Nanny somewhere in the back of the van. I wouldn't say it was your conventional road trip, Bob.

Ultimately, I decided not to attend the funeral, as I felt that it would just cause unnecessary drama. Amy informed me later that Princess sat on my mom's lap throughout the entire service and that one of my cousins served everyone Bud Light from a cooler in the back of his truck afterward. I feel certain that wasn't what Nanny had envisioned or wanted for her final re-membrance here on earth. But it serves as a reminder that your funeral isn't really one of those scenarios you can control.

I tell you this because it's the first memory that came to mind when Amy called me the Monday after Easter 2023. My mom's mental and physical health had been in a rapid decline over the past several years, and Amy had moved her from Oklahoma to an assisted-living facility in San Antonio about two years ear-lier. I need to stress how much I appreciate all that Amy did for our mom. She dealt with years of Suzanne being in and out of mental facilities, the highs and lows of her moods, her addic-tions, the venom she could spew, the death of James, and just generally not knowing what she would do at any given mo-ment. The decision to move her to San Antonio wasn't an easy one, but it's what needed to happen so Amy could keep an eye on her.

Caroline had just left to drive back to school after a long Easter weekend, so my heart was full as I answered the phone and heard Amy's voice. She began, "Mel, I'm just calling to let you know that I took Mom to the doctor a few weeks ago be-cause she's had some sores in her mouth that aren't getting bet-ter. They biopsied them and called to let me know it's a very aggressive cancer." I held my breath as she continued: "Because she's already in such bad health, they don't think there are any viable treatment options. The doctor said she probably only has one to two months to live. I just wanted you to know."

There are some moments that catch you by surprise no mat-ter how much you think you've prepared for them.

I thanked Amy for letting me know and then asked, "Do you think I should go see her?"

Amy replied, "I think that's totally up to you. You have to do what you think is best."

And let me tell you that I had no idea at that moment what that was. On the one hand, I'd accepted long ago that making the decision to walk away from that relationship might mean I'd never get the chance to say goodbye. But on the other hand, now I had that opportunity if I wanted it. I prayed over the next several weeks that God would give me specific direction as to what I should do, because I also didn't want to cause my mom any more pain at that stage in her life. I kept saying to God, "I'm at peace with her. I have peace about this situation." And what I believe He was saying back to me was "This isn't about your peace. It's about hers."

That was my answer.

I was at a point in my life where I was healed and whole. I could go see my mom if it meant it would bring her peace. It wasn't about me; it was about her. I called Amy to let her know I wanted to see Mom and asked if she would go with me. I was scared to see her after so many years—scared of regret, scared that she would lash out at me, scared that all the ways I'd felt healed over the past thirteen years would dissipate in an instant. I kept telling everyone around me that I was totally fine going to see her this last time, but really I felt unbelievably fragile.

I drove to Amy's house and picked her up. Then we drove to the assisted-living facility where my mom had been living for the past two years, and we sat in the parking lot for a few minutes. Amy did her best to prepare me, telling me Mom had been increasingly incoherent so she had no idea what we were walking into. She also informed me that Mom had called her over the weekend and asked, "Do you have an estimated time as to my demise?" which caused us both to laugh for a minute because the drama felt on brand.

I took a deep breath and told Amy I was nervous. She asked if I wanted her to pray for me, and I nodded. She reached over, grabbed my hand, and prayed the sweetest prayer for peace. Then we made our way from the car to the elevator to the room on the second floor where Mom was lying in a hospital bed. Hospice had been called in, and they seemed to think she probably wouldn't make it through the week. And as I walked into her room, I could see why. She was a shell of the woman I remembered.

The thing about my mom is that she was always beautiful. So when I followed Amy into the room, I was shocked by the old woman with gray hair who was lying there asleep in a hospital bed. She was painfully frail after fighting the cancer that was overtaking her body.

Amy quietly walked over to her and gently shook her awake. "You have a visitor. Do you want to wake up and see?" At that moment, I watched as Mom attempted to sit up in bed while her eyes lit up in recognition that her older daughter had finally come to see her after all the years of being apart. I'd realized over the past thirteen years that, in many ways, she'd done the best she could. She suffered from mental illness long before people really knew how to treat the highs and lows of bipolar disorder. And I believe that, in spite of all the ways she hurt me, she loved me as much as she was capable of loving someone. She was broken.

Amy raised her to a sitting position while I stood there awkwardly, not knowing what was going to happen next. Would my mom want to rehash all the whys of my walking away from our relationship all those years ago? Would it be another instance where I reached out, only to get hurt again as all the old, buried things floated to the surface like garbage during a flood?

There was no turning back, but I had zero idea what to say or do. Then Mom motioned for me to sit next to her and for Amy to sit on her other side. As we did our best to find room next to her on the narrow bed, she patted us and said, "Both of my girls are here. Both of my girls." There was so much love in her voice that it kind of levels me even now to think about it. She immediately followed that with "Look how beautiful you both are!" since physical appearance was always such a high priority in her life. Then she held my hand, and I watched as she tried to find her words amid the morphine and the pain and the emotion of the moment. Looking right at me, she finally said, "Sometimes we just need some time to work things out."

It was one of the most grace-filled moments of my life, as if God Himself gave her exactly the right thing to say in that moment. I was expecting blame, anger, and guilt; instead, she let me know that somewhere she understood that I'd done what I needed to do.

Then, as if no time had passed, she said, "Tell me what you've been up to."

So I gave her an overview of the past thirteen years of my life. I raised a child; I wrote some books; I sent my baby off to college.

While we sat there, Amy told me the story of Mom's last wild adventure, which had taken place just a few weeks before she was diagnosed with terminal sarcoma (and definitely in the throes of dementia). Normally, Mom and her friend Barb, who also lived in the assisted-living community, liked to sit out in the courtyard and smoke at various points throughout the day. I guess one afternoon they got bored and decided they wanted to bust out of the joint. Between the two of them, they figured out how to download the Uber app onto Mom's phone, used Barb's credit card, and ordered themselves a ride to Walmart. They spent the next four hours shopping every single aisle, trying on clothes, and riding around on a scooter until they realized it was probably time to get home—only they couldn't remember how to use Uber again. So at eight o'clock that evening, they called Amy to explain they "are at the Walmart and can't figure out how to get home." Amy's husband went to pick them up. He helped them load all their purchases into the car, drove them home, and carried their bags up to their rooms. While Amy told me this story and pointed out all the clothes from Walmart hanging in Mom's closet with price tags still on them, Mom just lay there with a grin on her face. It felt so fitting that her last act of defiance and adventure was a trip to Walmart. If ever there were a full-circle moment in a person's life, that would be it for her.

After about an hour, I could tell that Mom was starting to drift in and out of consciousness and needed to sleep. I held her hand, the hand that was still as familiar to me as my own, and said, "I love you, Mom." Because it's the truth. Love was never the problem.

She opened her eyes, looked at me, and said, "It's bulls and blood. It's the dust and mud."[1]

So what I'm telling you is that the last words my mom ever spoke to me were from the song "Rodeo" by Garth Brooks.

It kind of seems fitting, given our relationship. For years, we clashed; we fought; we hurt each other in numerous ways. We both carried scars from marks the other had left on us and walked away with permanent limps. And there came a point where the only thing I could do to survive was to get out of the arena.

A few days after my visit, Mom died. I woke up to a text from Amy letting me know she'd passed away at about three o'clock that morning. Amy had tried to call me, but I guess my phone decided I didn't need that call, even though I'd set my phone to let her calls bypass the Do Not Disturb feature. It's a weird thing to wake up and find out that your mom is no longer in this world, even though I knew it was a call I'd get soon and even though she hadn't been part of my life for more than a decade. The fact that I even got to say goodbye to her is a picture of God's grace, because I didn't know if I'd ever get that chance when I walked away from our relationship. I'd made a tremulous peace with that possibility years before. Despite that, I spent the day weighed down by an unspecified grief. The complexities of losing a parent are multifaceted in the best of circumstances, and this was so much more complicated. There was a sadness—not so much for the death itself, but for the grief and weight of what could have been, what should have been.

Sometimes we just need some time to work things out.

CHAPTER 20

Slaying the Dragons

I don't know why it continues to surprise me when I see God go before me in a situation and put pieces together in ways that I couldn't have planned if I'd tried. Sometimes I feel like maybe Jesus was talking to me personally when He said in Matthew 17:17, "How long shall I stay with you? How long shall I put up with you?" To be fair, they're valid questions. I can be the worst.

Like Perry says, "We aren't really even that good with Jesus, so how bad would we be without Him?" (This is where I also want to tell you that Perry would like to eventually host his own podcast called *This May Hurt a Little*, where he has guests on and tells them the truth about what's really wrong with them.)

My mom died on a Wednesday morning in May. Months before I even knew she was sick, I'd booked a vacation trip to Jackson Hole, Wyoming, with Perry and Caroline. At the time, I thought I chose those dates because it was during a small window of time that Caroline was out of school. But as it turns out, I chose those dates because God knew what was coming. The timing of this trip—we left the day after my mom passed away—was impeccable and exactly what my heart needed.

Grief is complicated, and mine was compounded by the fact that I wasn't even sure if I had a right to grieve. I'd been so careful to never talk about my relationship with my mom in public, so there was no way I was going to put up a social media post to let people know she'd died. I texted a few of my closest friends who knew the messy details of that relationship, but I didn't even know how I wanted them to respond. A couple of friends dropped off some snacks, and one dear friend had the most beautiful flowers delivered with a note that simply read, "My heart is so tender toward you today." It was the perfect thing to say. My own heart was so tender toward myself that day. It's like I was trying to comfort the little-girl version of myself who had truly lost her mother so many years ago.

We spent the day packing, which was a nice distraction. There is nothing like trying to make sure three large suitcases each fall under the fifty-pound weight limit to take your mind off bigger issues, especially when you have a husband who wants to pack his own fishing supplies and multiple pairs of hiking boots. Perry and Caroline would occasionally stop, look at me, and ask, "Are you okay?" and I would reply, "Yes, I think so," because I didn't really know if I was okay or not. I kept waiting for the dam to break.

Our flight was leaving at the crack of dawn the next morning. After we packed, I began to straighten up the house because I have a strict policy about coming home to a clean house post-vacation. I saw the flowers that had been delivered earlier sitting on my kitchen island and decided I hated for them to go to waste. I texted our neighbors who live across the street and asked, "Do y'all want some flowers? They were delivered today and we're leaving town tomorrow. I'd love for y'all to have them." They responded that they'd love them, so I picked up the vase and headed across the street.

When my neighbor opened the door, he said, "These are gorgeous! What were they for?"

Well. This feels awkward.

"Um, well, a friend sent them to me because my mom died," I said. It felt surreal to say it out loud.

"Oh my gosh," he replied. "I'm so sorry to hear that."

"Thank you. It's kind of weird. Our relationship was complicated. We didn't really speak," I explained, mainly because I didn't want him to feel sadness for me that should be reserved for people who had better relationships with their moms.

He nodded knowingly as he said, "Yes, family dynamics can be hard." Then he asked about our trip and how long we'd be gone.

We chatted for a bit until I said goodbye and headed back across the street. A few minutes later, my phone dinged with an incoming text message from his wife, who had sent the loveliest message. She is a deeply spiritual person and shared that she'd prayed over the flowers. She prayed that my mom was at peace, that I was at peace, that any lingering bitterness and resentment were gone, and that even now my mom was whole and healed in God's presence. It was her words, so comforting and just perfect, that caused the tears I'd tried to hold in all day to run down my face.

Whole and healed.

It's all I really ever wanted for myself. It's all I ever wanted for my mom.

And now I knew she finally was.

. . . . . .

Perry, Caroline, and I flew out the next morning. We landed at the airport in Jackson Hole, went to the rental-car kiosk, and then headed out the door. The Jackson Hole airport is in Grand Teton National Park, so the moment you walk outside, you're greeted with the sight of the majestic Tetons. It took our breath away.

We loaded our suitcases into our car and drove into town to check in to our hotel. After we freshened up from our day of travel, we decided we wanted to get back in the car and drive around in search of wildlife. This is basically Perry's favorite activity of all time, and he truly is like a wildlife whisperer. Earlier, when we'd left the airport, we drove past a river and he said, "If I were a moose, I'd be right next to that river." And suddenly there was a moose right next to that river. He's basically Marlin Perkins.

In the hope of seeing elk, mountain goats, and perhaps another moose or two, we started down a stretch of road that would lead us into the Bridger-Teton National Forest. As we drove, Caroline told us a story she'd been waiting to tell us face-to-face. During the spring semester at school, she'd been dealing with an issue with a leader in an organization she was involved in. There had been a lot of toxic behavior, and it had created some really hard situations, but as she told us parts of the story we hadn't heard yet, she said, "I finally spoke up because that behavior was affecting everyone else and a group is only as strong as its weakest person. I cared too much about the people around me to let that behavior continue unchecked."

In that moment, God showed me that Caroline had the discernment to see an unhealthy situation clearly and that once she saw it, she didn't care what it cost to speak up. She wasn't afraid to use her voice to advocate for herself and others to try to make the situation healthy.

She'd fought the dragon.

And she knew how to fight the dragon because she'd fought other dragons.

I didn't know it all those years ago when I rocked this same little girl to sleep, but this had always been the goal. As a young mom, I believed it was my job to protect her. What I didn't realize was that I could do my best and bad things were still going to happen. It's part of life. We live in a broken world, full of broken people.

God revealed to me over the ensuing years the parts of my heart that needed to be healed, the ways I needed to trust Him more, and how to see myself as He saw me instead of focusing on my perceived inadequacies. He knew I was going to be able to raise a warrior only if I learned how to be strong so I could show her the way. And as I heard Caroline telling us how she'd taken a stand, I realized God had broken a generational cycle that had told the women in my family to find their value in everything but His love.

Once we reached an overlook, Caroline and Perry jumped out of the car to go look for elk. I walked behind them as Perry put his arm around Caroline while the sun began to set behind the mountains. I started to cry as I realized the extent of the gift of being in this place, at this time, with this family that was

God's redemption of so much of the hurt I'd had in my life. This was my dream right here in front of me, and I felt nothing but gratitude for every single bit of it. Like everything else in life, it isn't perfect, but it's filled with so much grace and goodness.

And I saw in that moment that every dragon we'd fought had been worth it. I also knew there will always be more dragons ahead. But I rest in knowing that we can trust the One who fights for us and with us. And that I've raised a daughter who knows the same.

God is within her, she will not fall.

—Psalm 46:5

ACKNOWLEDGMENTS

I always knew the day would come when I would write this particular book and talk publicly about my relationship with my mother and the effect it had on my life. I just didn't know *this* book was going to be *that* book until after I signed the contract. I had no idea my mom would end up passing away just a couple of months later, which gave me the freedom to tell *this* story at *this* time. Only God could have orchestrated the timing of it all, and it's a reminder to me that He is always writing a better story for us than anything we would write for ourselves. I'm so grateful for His love, His sovereignty, and the unfailing way He continues to put the pieces of my life together. My boundary lines have fallen in pleasant places (Psalm 16:6).

Being able to write and tell stories is the gift that keeps on giving, even as it is sometimes the very thing that makes me question my sanity. That being said, I'd like to thank my literary agent, Lisa Jackson, and the team at Alive for believing in me and being patient with me when I repeatedly say, "I don't think I have it in me to write another book," and then follow it up a few months later with "So, here's what I'm thinking for my next book. Will you help me?" The answer is always yes. Thanks for knowing me so well.

Thank you, too, to the editorial, marketing, sales, and publicity teams at WaterBrook. From our first phone call, I knew that y'all were a team that would have my back and help me make this book everything I hoped it could be. Special thanks to my editor, Susan Tjaden, who makes me a much better writer than I actually am and forced me to confront the fact that I use the word *honestly* way too much. You honestly are the best.

I'm forever grateful to my dear friend, business partner, and podcast co-host, Sophie Hudson. How different would my life look if God hadn't brought you into it all those years ago? Thank you for reading these pages long before anyone else did and letting me know when it sounds like I'm writing a novel about World War II instead of using my real writing voice. You lived a lot of this story with me, and your prayers and encouragement have truly changed my life in too many ways to count.

Everyone needs a bold truth-teller in their life, and one of those people for me is my friend and business manager, Retha. Thank you for holding my feet to the fire to get this book written and knowing when to push me and when to let me be. You make me a better person both professionally and personally.

To the women who follow me online and listen to *The Big Boo Cast*, most of whom I've never met in person. I just want to say thank you from the bottom of my heart. You've made my dreams a reality, and it makes me happy that there are people out there who know exactly what I mean when I say, "You only get one face." Thanks for reading and listening to my particular brand of nonsense all these years.

To the Birthday Club. Thank you for all the ways you've walked beside me on this journey. I'm so grateful for the way y'all have cheered me on, listened, and understood all the complexities of family dynamics because you've been there too. Never underestimate the healing power of some margaritas and laughter.

One of the biggest blessings of my life showed up at Texas A&M when I was nineteen years old. Gulley, you are my very heart and have lived this story with me. Thank you for always listening, always loving, and always being there to remind me to "Get excited, Coach Fran." Getting to raise our kids together has been one of my favorite adventures, and I can't wait to see what's next.

To Honey and Big. Thank you for all the ways you've loved me and supported me over the years. I know you were just using me in the hope I'd one day become an author and speaker who could get you into a luncheon for free, but I still appreciate you both so much for taking in a lost, scared nineteen-year-old girl all those years ago. And thanks for always leaving me the brownie edges.

To my mother-in-law, Sallie. Thank you for all the prayers I know you said for me as I wrote this book. And thank you for raising Perry to be a man of faith and integrity.

To my dad and Cherrie, who have so graciously allowed me to tell this story. Thank you. The two of you have loved me through all my highs and lows. You've seen me at my best and at my worst. You've been the best Bops and Mimi to Caroline, and I'm grateful for all the ways you continue to show up for all of us. We are the luckiest to have you both.

To my little sister, Amy. What can I say? We lived every bit of this together, and there were times when I thought it might tear us apart. I'm so appreciative of the way you've always worked to understand my perspective and love me even when we may not agree. I'm also grateful beyond words for the way you took care of Mom in the last years of her life. It was a heavy burden to carry, and you did it with grace and love. Thank you for that and for letting me write this story.

To my sweet (and a little salty) Caroline. Raising you and seeing the woman you've become has been the greatest gift of my entire life. You are God's redemption and beauty for ashes in my life. I'm so proud of the way you never fail to fight dragons and walk the path God has for you, even when it costs you. You are my hero, and I hope I've taught you even half as much as you've taught me. I love you more than I can say. I can't wait to see all the things God has for you as you walk into the future.

And to Perry. You are the man I prayed and hoped for. "Thank you" doesn't seem like enough for the innumerable ways you have challenged me, loved me, and shaped my life. You have battled with me as we created a new generational legacy, and I am so fortunate that you are mine. You are home to me.

NOTES

INTRODUCTION

1. Bon Jovi, "Livin' on a Prayer," by Jon Bon Jovi, Richie Sambora, and Desmond Child, *Slippery When Wet*, Mercury Records, 1986.

CHAPTER 4: MY FIRST MEAN GIRL

1. Taylor Swift, "Anti-Hero," by Taylor Swift and Jack Antonoff, *Midnights*, Republic, 2022.

CHAPTER 5: THE TRUTH OF IT ALL

1. *Gone with the Wind*, directed by Victor Fleming (Culver City, Calif.: Selznick International Pictures, 1939).

CHAPTER 6: LIKE RAIN ON YOUR WEDDING DAY

Chapter 6 takes its name, "Like Rain on Your Wedding Day," from the song "Ironic." Alanis Morissette, *Jagged Little Pill*, Maverick Recording Company, 1995.

1. Jerry Reed, "East Bound and Down," by Jerry Reed and Deena Kaye Rose, *Smokey and the Bandit* (Original Motion Picture Soundtrack), Geffen Records, 1977.

CHAPTER 8: SWEET CAROLINE

Chapter 8 takes its name, "Sweet Caroline," from the song with the same title. Neil Diamond, *Brother Love's Travelling Salvation Show*, Geffen Records, 1969.

CHAPTER 13: HEALING BELOW THE SURFACE

1. *Mean Girls*, directed by Mark Waters (Hollywood, Calif.: Paramount Pictures, 2004).
2. *Redeeming Love*, directed by D. J. Caruso (Universal City, Calif.: Universal Pictures, 2022).

CHAPTER 14: YOU CAN'T SIT AT OUR TABLE

1. *Seinfeld*, season 9, episode 3, "The Serenity Now," directed by Andy Ackerman, written by Steve Koren, featuring Jerry Seinfeld, Julia Louis-Dreyfus, and Michael Richards, aired October 9, 1997, on NBC, www.imdb.com/title/tt0697773.

CHAPTER 15: CARRYING YOUR OWN BUCKET

1. G. Michael Hopf, *Those Who Remain: A Postapocalyptic Novel*, The New World Series (self-pub., 2016), 18.

CHAPTER 16: STOPPING THE MEAN-GIRL CYCLE

1. "U.S. Teen Girls Experiencing Increased Sadness and Violence," Centers for Disease Control and Prevention, February 13, 2023, www.cdc.gov/media/releases/2023/p0213-yrbs.html.

CHAPTER 17: GO MAKE SOMETHING OF YOURSELF, KID

1. *The Electric Horseman*, directed by Sydney Pollack (Universal City, Calif.: Universal Pictures, 1979).

CHAPTER 19: BULLS AND BLOOD, THE DUST AND MUD

1. Garth Brooks, "Rodeo," by Larry Bastian, *Ropin' the Wind*, Capitol Nashville, 1991.

ABOUT THE AUTHOR

MELANIE SHANKLE is a three-time *New York Times* bestselling author and speaker. She is also the co-host of *The Big Boo Cast,* a weekly podcast with her friend Sophie Hudson. They started the podcast in 2007, which is pretty remarkable for two people who didn't even fully understand what a podcast was at that time. They now average close to forty thousand listeners per week and still find it hard to believe that anyone wants to listen to what they have to say.

Melanie is the author of multiple books, including *Nobody's Cuter than You, Church of the Small Things,* and *On the Bright Side.* She also has a hundred-day devotional for women titled *Everyday Holy,* a hundred-day devotional for teen girls called *Fearless Faith,* and a children's picture book, *Piper and Mabel: Two Very Wild but Very Good Dogs.*

Melanie is a 1993 graduate of Texas A&M. She lives in San Antonio with her husband, Perry. Her daughter, Caroline, is a proud member of the Texas A&M class of 2025.

In her free time, Melanie likes to shop and do her part to keep retailers in business. She attends as many Texas A&M sporting events as she can, because hope springs eternal. And most days, you can find her walking Piper and Mabel, because it's their world and she's just living in it.

ABOUT THE TYPE

This book was set in Caslon, a typeface first designed in 1722 by William Caslon (1692–1766). Its widespread use by most English printers in the early eighteenth century soon supplanted the Dutch typefaces that had formerly prevailed. The roman is considered a "workhorse" typeface due to its pleasant, open appearance, while the italic is exceedingly decorative.